in·'te·gri·ty

[principles of christian ethics]

in·'te·gri·ty

principles of christian ethics

WORD AFLAME PRESS
WELDON SPRING, MO

RICHARD M. DAVIS

Word Aflame Press
36 Research Park Court, Weldon Spring, MO 63304
pentecostalpublishing.com

Cover design by Elizabeth Loyd

26 25 24 23 22 21 20 19 18 17   1 2 3 4 5

Library of Congress Cataloging-in-Publication Data

Names: Davis, Richard M., 1953- author.
Title: Integrity : principles of Christian ethics / By Richard M. Davis.
Description: Weldon Spring : Word Aflame Press, 2016.
Identifiers: LCCN 2016046187 (print) | LCCN 2016046785 (ebook) | ISBN
  9780757752285 (alk. paper) | ISBN 9780757752308 (spanish : alk. paper) |
  ISBN 9780757752292 () | ISBN 9780757752315 (Spanish)
Subjects: LCSH: Christian ethics.
Classification: LCC BJ1251 .D29 2016 (print) | LCC BJ1251 (ebook) | DDC
  241--dc23
LC record available at https://lccn.loc.gov/2016046187

To Sharon, my beloved wife,

a companion of profound Christian ethics.

To my daughters

Sharilyn, Andrea, Marla,

and your husbands Trent, Keith, and Tim.

I dedicate this work to you and to our grandchildren

in the interest of a more ethical world

in which to live, love, and work.

Contents

INTRODUCTION

hon·est *adj.* **1.** Marked by or displaying integrity; upright. **2.** Not deceptive or fraudulent; genuine. **3.** Equitable; fair. **4.a.** Characterized by truth; not false. **b.** Sincere; frank. **5.a.** Of good repute; respectable. **b.** Without affectation; plain. **6.** Virtuous; chaste.

in·teg·ri·ty *n.* **1.** Steadfast adherence to a strict moral or ethical code. **2.** The state of being unimpaired; soundness. **3.** The quality or condition of being whole or undivided; completeness.

The whole purpose of Christianity is to redeem fallen humankind. In his unregenerate and fallen state a person is selfish and corrupt. He thinks chiefly of himself and cares little if at all about the fate and destiny of others. Only the regenerating power of Jesus Christ can redeem the soul of an individual and elevate him to the higher plane of abundant life. The love of Christ can transform a person and change him from a thoughtless, self-serving individual into a selfless, caring ambassador of the love of God.

Jesus Christ was God manifested in flesh, the Son of God. He fully knew and understood the frailty of human flesh, for He was tempted in every way we are tempted, yet He was without sin (Hebrews 4:15). He experienced the full gamut of human suffering and temptation, yet He lived the authentic human life with complete victory and in flawless, divine perfection. Because Christ lived in victory and overcame the temptations of the world, He now lives in us through the Holy Spirit, sustaining and empowering believers with spiritual victory. (See John 16:33; Philippians 4:13.)

Still, we are human beings and are subject to failure in the flesh when we live according to our fleshly whims and desires. Those who walk according to their flesh are carnal. Carnal people stumble and fail, and in their carnal living they displease God. Only as we walk in the Spirit and seek to live a spiritual life that is pleasing to God are we certain of spiritual victory and the absence of fleshly condemnation. (See Romans 8:1–8.)

True Christianity involves individuals who choose to emulate Jesus Christ and live by spiritual values. True Christians choose not to pursue a carnal and self-serving lifestyle, oblivious to the welfare of others. To be a Christian is to be kind and to love and care about others as Jesus Christ has loved and cared for us.

The principles of Christianity—the principles given to us and demonstrated by Jesus Christ Himself—comprise the highest and best lifestyle a person can live. To live by the high principles of Christ is to live an edifying lifestyle of service to our fellow man. These life-changing principles are the foundation of Christian ethics.

One of the greatest needs in our society is the need for people to live by ethical principles of conduct. We could resolve and avoid many conflicts and misunderstandings through practicing ethical behavior that is based in the loving and caring Spirit of Christ Jesus. And where could we possibly gain a clearer understanding of ethical principles than from the life and ministry of Jesus Christ and the church He established some two millennia ago?

The *American Heritage Dictionary* defines the word *ethic* as "a set of principles of right conduct; a theory or a system of moral values." *Ethics* is "the study of the general nature of morals and of the specific moral choices to be made by a person; moral philosophy; the rules or standards governing the conduct of a person or the members of a profession."

Every profession has a code of ethics, whether it is a formal, written philosophy of standards or an informal, unwritten code for behavior. It is the code of conduct accepted by the members of that profession that brings continuity, confidence, and harmony to the common cause and effort of the whole. However, ethical behavior is not reserved for the exclusive use of professional groups and institutions. Every individual should live by a code of ethical principles.

Christians glean their code of ethics from the Scriptures. To live by the principles of God's Word is to live by the highest moral and ethical code revealed to humankind. The Bible gives guidance to our lives for every situation of life by providing basic principles of moral behavior.

Contrary to what many people would like to believe, ethical behavior is foundational and fundamental to godly living. There is no such thing as what many people refer to as "situation ethics." Situations do not govern or alter true ethical conduct.

Rather, the true ethical principles taught by God's Word will guide us through every situation. Ethical principles are certain, unchanging, and enduring. Like coastal lighthouses warn and guide mariners through the dangerous waters, ethical principles guide us through the uncertain waters of human relationships.

Once discovered and understood, we can rely on principles of ethical conduct to guide us through whatever perils and questions we may face in life's journey. The principles of God's Word not only will guide us, but also strengthen us for the journey.

There also are practical reasons to undertake this study of Christian ethics. Believe it or not, sometime in your life you may be accused of being unethical or disloyal, and the accusation will sting. Unfortunately, life brings with it conflicts—and conflict brings differences of opinion, misunderstandings, and disagreements. Whenever the wound of such a charge strikes against your soul and spirit, you need to know without doubt you have lived in such a way that completely repudiates the charge. If everyone lived by the code of Christ's ethics, there would be few instances of disharmony, and in those rare situations individuals would quickly endeavor to reach a common understanding with love and kindness toward each other. Christ taught this approach, and we should follow it.

We simply should live in such an ethical and loving Christian way that people will refuse to believe our critics.

CHAPTER ONE

THE FOUNDATION OF ETHICS — CREATED IN THE IMAGE OF GOD

A son honoureth his father, and a servant his master: if then I be a father, where is mine honour? and if I be a master, where is my fear? saith the LORD of hosts unto you, O priests, that despise my name. And ye say, Wherein have we despised thy name? (Malachi 1:6)

Now unto the King eternal, immortal, invisible, the only wise God, be honour and glory for ever and ever. Amen. (I Timothy 1:17)

Knowing and maintaining proper ethics is a problem in our world. It is not only a problem among Christians; it is a problem among all people and relationships.

In their article "CEOs stumble over ethics violations, mismanagement," authors Gary Strauss and Laura Petrecca of *USA Today* introduced several ethical problems among prominent CEOs:

> Yahoo CEO Scott Thompson lasted just four months before revelations of résumé padding forced him to resign. . . . Best Buy Chairman and founder Richard Schulze exited . . . after directors determined he used poor judgment for failing to disclose CEO Brian Dunn's personal relationship with a young subordinate. . . . And JPMorgan Chase CEO Jamie Dimon is under fire after the investment bank's $2.3 billion trading blunder. (*USA Today*, May 15, 2012, accessed June 30, 2016)

In every nation, among every people, and in every human endeavor people often fail to live by the appropriate level of ethics. In examining the topic of ethics and how to cultivate the highest possible standards of conduct, where should one begin? Perhaps we could look back to the origins of humankind for a point of beginning.

That humankind was created in the image of God seems an appropriate place to begin a study of ethics. When a person recognizes the Creator and that all mankind was created in the image of that Creator, it will affect how the individual views and treats his or her fellow man. We respect God who created us; that same respect logically should extend to our fellow man who also was created in the same image of God. Consequently, our creation in His image appears as the foundation for human ethics.

It is easy enough for Christians to agree this is the foundation for human ethics. However, some people have not come to terms with their origins and have not embraced the Creator. Still, they possess a sense of right and wrong when it comes to how they interact with and treat their fellow man. Further, even Christians who possess knowledge of the Creator look for specific guidelines to assist them in keeping their conduct with others on an appropriate level. To what might a person look for such guidance?

A Christian will look first and foremost to the Holy Scriptures—the Word of God—when seeking principles to govern his treatment of others, and rightfully so. But are there guiding principles that extend even to nonbelievers who desire to treat others with due respect? Even though most ethical conduct is not a matter of obeying rigid laws, we also could look to governing laws and their foundations to discover fundamental principles to guide one's ethical conduct.

When the United States was founded over two centuries ago, the foundation for the new nation's legal systems flowed primarily out of the system of English Common Law with which the founders were most familiar. Of the various influences that contributed to the Common Law, the greatest influence was undoubtedly that of the Mosaic law and ecclesiastical law. One could accurately say the Mosaic law forms most of the foundation of US law.

> Professor Silving [Helen Silving, Professor of Law of the University of Puerto Rico] maintains that many old legal documents of the Western culture may have their origins in the Bible. "It is remarkable, indeed, and has an interesting

bearing on the nature of our reactions to the Bible, that this has passed unnoticed, while efforts have been made to connect our constitutional documents with Greek and Roman ideas."

Consequently, English common law reflects the Biblical Scriptural heritage of the Western civilization.

Eugen Rosenstock-Huessy, author of "Out of Revolution, Autobiography of Western Man" declared, "Common law was Christian law." (http://liberty-virtue-independence.blogspot.com/2008/12/foundation-of-english-common-law.html, accessed May 16, 2016)

Every civilized culture must have some basis upon which it establishes its codes of conduct, whether codified laws or principles of acceptable behavior. Any people group without such a foundation would be primitive and uncivilized, and anarchy would surely reign supreme. Consequently, every person—believer or nonbeliever—may look to the legal system for certain clues as to proper ethical behavior. Still, whether they know it or not, they are essentially looking to principles that came first from the pages of Scripture.

Further, although not every person has become a believer in Christ, God has placed within the heart of every individual a sense of divine connection. Some people may reject that inner sense or they may try to fulfill it through spiritual endeavors that fail to recognize the one true God. Still, practically every human possesses some degree of awareness of something greater than himself, a sense of awe for all creation.

For the Christian, one's awareness of something greater than oneself leads to a knowledge of and reverence for the Creator who made humankind. When an individual comes to know the Creator, the accompanying sense of awe and respect gives him a desire to acknowledge God and honor Him in everything he does. (See Proverbs 3:6.)

Every Christian desires to please God through all of life's daily activities. Likewise, God desires to receive honor and glory from the lives of His people. But God does not desire to receive honor in order to satisfy a need within Himself; the Lord is already filled with honor, for He is the essence of honor. His desire to receive honor is based upon humankind's need to acknowledge and honor Him. For example, consider the psalmist David.

David recognized the honor or glory of God and that God's glory is ever present within Him. Consequently, he associated the Tabernacle, or house of God, as the place where the honor or glory of God resided. David wrote, "O LORD, I love the habitation of your house and the place where your glory dwells. Do not sweep my soul away with sinners, nor my life with bloodthirsty men, in whose hands are evil devices, and whose right hands are full of bribes. But as for me, I shall walk in my integrity; redeem me, and be gracious to me" (Psalm 26:8–11, ESV).

What is honor? The *American Heritage Dictionary* defines the noun *honor* as "1. High respect, as that shown for special merit; esteem. 2.a. Good name; reputation. b. A source or cause of credit. 3.a. Glory or recognition; distinction. b. A mark, token, or gesture of respect or distinction. c. A military decoration. d. A title conferred for achievement. . . ."

God does not lack for honor; honor emanates from Him. It is an aspect of His nature. Consequently, God's desire for humankind to honor Him is not based in selfishness on His part. Rather, God has designed a special role for honor to fulfill in human life.

- Living an honorable life is an aspect of living the best life one can experience on earth.
- Giving honor is also the path to receiving honor.
- God has given to humankind a measure of honor as the highest order of all God's creative works.
- God desires to nurture and cultivate a growing presence and experience of honor in a person's life.
- Humans receiving honor in life ultimately return honor to God.
- Humans experience the highest possible measure of honor through salvation from sin—that God would love us enough to purchase our redemption.

When a person experiences salvation through Jesus Christ, he experiences relationship with Christ and enters into a lifestyle that ultimately honors God. Further, it is a lifestyle that also will bring honor to the individual. But before a person can experience salvation in Christ, the person must recognize the grandeur and worthiness of God to receive all glory and honor in everything. Like respect and love, honor is one of those things in life a person must give in order to receive it. Although a person may not fully comprehend the extent of God's greatness, he or she will fundamentally recognize that God is supremely worthy of honor above all things.

GOD—WORTHY OF HONOR

> Riches and honour are with me; yea, durable riches and righteousness. (Proverbs 8:18)

> Glory and honour are in his presence; strength and gladness are in his place. Give unto the LORD, ye kindreds of the people, give unto the LORD glory and strength. Give unto the LORD the glory due unto his name. . . . Let the heavens be glad, and let the earth rejoice. . . . O give thanks unto the LORD; for he is good; for his mercy endureth for ever. And say ye, Save us, O God of our salvation, and gather us together, and deliver us from the heathen, that we may give thanks to thy holy name, and glory in thy praise." (I Chronicles 16:27–35)

In the presence of God is glory and honor. To come into God's presence is to encounter His glory and holiness, and respect demands we give Him the glory and honor due Him.

We owe a great debt to God. He is our Creator; we would not exist were it not for His glorious power, and we could not continue to exist were it not for His supreme love and mercy. Some individuals try to live independent of the power and presence of God and they believe they owe nothing to any other person or being, but they are sadly mistaken. Humankind owes everything to God his Creator, but he especially owes God respect and honor.

Honor God by Being

The firmament of this earth declares the glory of God, for God has created the heavens and given to them their great glory (Psalm 19:1–6). How do the sun, moon, and stars give glory to God? They simply shine forth with the light God has given them. They honor God simply by *being* what He made them to be.

God also has created humankind to *be* vessels of honor unto Him. Whether or not a person honors God with his life, his existence honors God. As surely as the heavenly bodies declare the glory of God by their mere existence, humankind honors God in that fashion as well. In fact, the study of the marvelous human body is a study of the glory of God. As the psalmist poetically observed, we are "fearfully and wonderfully made" (Psalm 139:14). With incredible, balanced complexity, the human body is composed of various intricate systems that astound the student of physiology.

While all of creation praises the Creator by merely *being* what He has made them to be, He created humankind with an even higher purpose: to praise God not only by being, but also by *doing* as God directs.

Honor God by Doing

How does a person glorify and honor God? He simply lives his life as God has designed it—following a lifestyle that honors Christ in both worship and conduct.

> Make a joyful noise unto God, all ye lands: sing forth the honour of his name: make his praise glorious. Say unto God, How terrible art thou in thy works! through the greatness of thy power shall

> thine enemies submit themselves unto thee. All the
> earth shall worship thee, and shall sing unto thee;
> they shall sing to thy name. Selah. (Psalm 66:1–4)

To demonstrate the salvation of the Lord by living a redeemed lifestyle is the greatest act of praise and worship humankind can offer to God. (See Psalm 96:1–13.) When people are redeemed from the ravages of sinful living, they have a new song of joy and contentment in their hearts and on their lips. They no longer desire to waste their lives with the sinful activities they once thrived upon. Rather, they desire to live in ways that give praise, glory, and honor to Jesus Christ.

> O worship the LORD in the beauty of holiness: fear
> before him, all the earth. (Psalm 96:9)

> Bless the LORD, O my soul. O LORD my God, thou
> art very great; thou art clothed with honour and
> majesty. (Psalm 104:1)

God is incontestably great! He created all things. What mortal could rationally question or deny His demonstrated greatness, which all may observe? True, at some point the acceptance of divine Creation becomes a matter of faith. However, what other explanation for the origins of creation and human life can compare? The intricacies of every life system on the planet declare God's glory.

Every beautiful view of the glorious majesties of nature shout out God's greatness. For instance, consider the majestic Guadalupe Peak standing tall and proud high above the salt flats of West Texas. Or contemplate the crystalline, white sands of Miramar Beach near Destin, Florida. Not only are the beaches of the Florida Panhandle breathtaking in their beauty, but God also knows the number of the grains of sand in each one of them. Can anyone deny the beauty of the moon in its full stage, shining upon the earth like a sentinel in the night? The stellar beauties of the universe cry out His glory!

All observable systems of the earth declare the glory of God as they simply exist, doing that which He created them to do. How can humankind—the most intelligent of all His creation—deny His glory?

Think about it. Every intricately designed invention declares its creator—that an intelligent, creative being brought it about. Consider a clock hanging on the wall; its design empowers it to slowly, methodically track every second of every minute of every hour of the day. That could not just happen; someone designed and created it. A gasoline-powered automobile engine declares its inventor. How could such a marvelous piece of machinery just appear and begin to work with such mechanical precision and balance? It couldn't. The very thought is ludicrous. But it is just as absurd to view the intricacies of this beautiful world and assume it "just happened" through some unobservable process of evolution—and that over millions of years!

No! The heavens declare God's glory (Psalm 19:1) as they simply do what He has created them to do—hanging in their respective places, making their orderly orbits, shining out with beauty and glory. It is all to the glory of the divine Creator. And humankind should recognize and praise the Creator by both being and doing—that is, by doing all they can to acknowledge and honor Him as Creator!

The Almighty deserves the praises of all creation! There is none like Him. He created all things throughout the universe for His eternal pleasure. John the Revelator wrote, "Thou art worthy, O Lord, to receive glory and honour and power: for thou hast created all things, and for thy pleasure they are and were created" (Revelation 4:11).

MAN—CREATED TO GIVE HONOR TO GOD

Of all God's creation, humankind is the most intelligent and the one endowed with freewill and the power of choice. Yet of all creatures he is the one creation who often chooses to exercise his own stubborn plan in life and ignore his Creator. Paul addressed the sinful arrogance of humankind in the first chapter of his epistle to the believers in Rome:

> For the invisible things of him from the creation of the world are clearly seen, being understood by the things that are made, even his eternal power and Godhead; so that they are without excuse: because that, when they knew God, they glorified him not as God, neither were thankful; but became vain in their imaginations, and their foolish heart was darkened. Professing themselves to be wise, they became fools. (Romans 1:20–22)

Mankind was not just born—he was created! To say that one was born is a true statement, but it fails to tell the whole story. To speak of birth only focuses on the human element of procreation, or that which man does to produce life through bearing offspring. But the subject of mankind's origin is much greater and far more encompassing than only his ability to reproduce after his own kind. God created humankind and gave him the ability to procreate. Each living person has by his birth a link to the eternal, creative, and divine nature of God through the Creation and through man's God-given ability to reproduce. We are created to bring honor and glory to the eternal God! (See Proverbs 3:1–10; Revelation 4:11.)

Only as we learn to honor God with the substance of our lives (Proverbs 3:9) are we able to know the real meaning of abundant life. What is honoring God with our substance? We think of material substance since the next phrase of Proverbs 3:9 mentions "the firstfruits of all thine increase" and verse 10 addresses material increases. Without question, we are to honor God with our material substance, including the firstfruits of our increase, or the first tenth—the tithe. But the wise writer of the Book of Proverbs touched upon much more than only honoring God with our money and possessions.

A life of true substance goes far beyond monetary and economic considerations. The substance of a person's life involves the areas of significance in his life. When we bless and honor God in every area of our life, we are honoring Him with our substance, and the end result for us will be an abundant life in Jesus Christ!

For example, consider two verses in the New Testament where the word *substance* appears:

> And Joanna the wife of Chuza Herod's steward, and Susanna, and many others, which ministered unto him of their substance. (Luke 8:3)

> And not many days after the younger son gathered all together, and took his journey into a far country, and there wasted his substance with riotous living. (Luke 15:13)

Those who ministered "of their substance" gave much more to the Lord Jesus than their physical possessions; they gave of their time and of their lives. And the prodigal son wasted much more valuable substance in riotous living than only his monetary inheritance; he wasted part of his life. He may have worked hard later in life and possibly was able to replace the physical substance he had squandered. However, there was an invaluable part of his life he would never recoup; it was forever gone, wasted, and spent, never to return.

We should be good stewards of the physical wealth God has entrusted to us, but we also should be good stewards of the real substance of life—love, peace, friendship, and joy to name only a few. We are created to honor God with the substance of our lives in service to Him and to others. We honor Him in our life, in our death, and in eternity.

Created to Serve

It is amazing that in modern North American culture many people seek to be served rather than to serve others. God created us to serve others from a pure heart. The loss of a spirit of servanthood is at the root of many of North America's most desperate ills. Crowded jails and overburdened court systems reflect a self-seeking society that seeks personal gratification at the expense of others. It is a spirit that says, "Whatever it takes, I will get what I want, and I don't care who I hurt in the process!"

Although self-centeredness is a disease at the core of North American values, it is neither a new problem nor one exclusive to America. It was also at the root of the thieves' hearts who attacked the "certain man" on his way to Jericho. They robbed and beat him with the attitude, "What's yours is mine and I'm going to take it." Almost as selfish as the robbers were the priest and the Levite, who each in turn passed by the desperately needy man, pitied him, and went on their way without lending assistance. Their self-centered attitude was one of noninvolvement: "What's mine is mine, and I'm going to keep it."

Fortunately, there was one man who encountered the broken man in his pitiful state and had mercy on him. The good man was a Samaritan, a people of mixed race who generally were despised at worst or disrespected at best. Still, he stopped to help. The good Samaritan, as he has come to be known, reached out like a servant to help his fellow man. His attitude suggested, "What's mine is not mine at all; I'm going to share it."

Jesus Christ did not come to be served, although He of all people is most worthy to be served with honor. Rather, Jesus Christ came as a servant reaching out to His creation: "Let nothing be done through strife or vainglory; but in lowliness of mind let each esteem other better than themselves. Look not every man on his own things, but every man also on the things of others. Let this mind be in you, which was also in Christ Jesus: who, being in the form of God, thought it not robbery to be equal with God: but made himself of no reputation, and took upon him the form of a servant, and was made in the likeness of men: and being found in fashion as a man, he humbled himself, and became obedient unto death, even the death of the cross" (Philippians 2:3–8). (See also I Thessalonians 4:4; I Timothy 6:1–21; Hebrews 3:1–6.)

We were created for the purpose of serving others in the name of Jesus Christ, and when we do we bring honor to the name and person of Christ. As servants we live a lifestyle that honors the Lord Jesus Christ and we discover what true life is all about.

Created to Live

Not only are we created to serve, but also to discover and experience a full and satisfying life. We are created to live a life of spiritual abundance. Although we may be poor by this world's monetary standards, we can live with the abundance of which Jesus spoke (John 10:10). Indeed, life does not consist of the possessions one may accumulate (Luke 12:15), but of our searching out the kingdom of God and living by God's kingdom principles. That is real living!

I recently read an account of a homeless man who was on his knees in the street, praying and giving thanks. When someone asked him why a homeless man with nothing would be thanking God, He replied, "I might not have much in material things, but I have the greatest gift of all—salvation—thanks to Jesus Christ! My riches don't come from man and money, but from our heavenly Father!" He was homeless, yet rich.

> He that followeth after righteousness and mercy
> findeth life, righteousness, and honour.
> (Proverbs 21:21)
>
> By humility and the fear of the LORD are riches,
> and honour, and life. (Proverbs 22:4)

We are created to live by the power and love of Jesus Christ. When His love is resplendent in our heart by His resident Holy Spirit, then we can experience the fullest life with contentment and satisfaction. But before we can live in Christ, we must die to our carnal desires. We not only are created to live, but we also are created to die.

Created to Die

It is only possible to please God through faith, and carnality works against faith. *Carnal* means "fleshly," so in literal terms we all are carnal. However, in context, to be carnal is to walk and live by fleshly desires and understanding. The Scriptures teach us that carnality assures us only of spiritual death, but to live by a spiritual mindset assures us of life in Christ (Romans 8:6). We must first die before we can experience full spiritual life—die to our own selfish and sinful desires, which are carnal.

We honor God by living according to His Holy Spirit. That is the spiritual life of which the apostle Paul wrote in Romans 8. It is a life of righteousness, peace, and joy in the Spirit, and it is abundant life lived as the sons and daughters of God (Romans 8:6, 14).

It is insufficient to honor God only with our lips—that is, with our words and profession. (See Isaiah 29:13.) We must serve Him from a regenerated heart that has been transformed by the power of His Spirit. When we have died to our sinful nature, we can live in the Spirit!

> Ye hypocrites, well did Esaias prophesy of you, saying, This people draweth nigh unto me with their mouth, and honoureth me with their lips; but their heart is far from me. But in vain they do worship me, teaching for doctrines the commandments of men. (Matthew 15:7–9)

MAN—CREATED TO RECEIVE HONOR

By living a lifestyle that honors Jesus Christ, we discover and experience God's highest purpose for mankind. Further, we will receive honor from God and from our fellow man. It is God's intention not only to receive honor from humankind, but also to give honor to him. If we honor God, He will honor us and make us His special people!

> Wherefore the Lord God of Israel saith, I said indeed that thy house, and the house of thy father, should walk before me for ever: but now the Lord saith, Be it far from me; for them that honour me I will honour, and they that despise me shall be lightly esteemed. (I Samuel 2:30)
>
> (See also Deuteronomy 26:16–19.)

The apostle Peter wrote that Christians are a peculiar, or special (New King James Version), people—a prized possession and the apple of His eye (I Peter 2:9; Psalm 17:8). When God created humankind He gave him special glory and honor as His highest creation. He gave mankind dominion over all the works of His hands. (See Psalm 8:5–6; Hebrews 2:7.) But God had a higher level of honor and blessing in mind for His special people. Not only had He created them in His image and given them honor and dominion, but He also had a plan to fill them with a personal, abiding presence of His Holy Spirit. What a distinct honor and glory to be filled with the Spirit of the Almighty!

God has given believers the greatest honor of all by indwelling their hearts through the Holy Spirit. Because He lives within us, we have power to experience life in its most potent and fulfilling measure—life abundant. As we enjoy the abundant life Christ designed for His church, we are honoring God in the way that pleases Him the most—by *being* the people He made us to be and by *doing* the things He has called us to do. We are living a lifestyle that honors the name and person of the Lord Jesus Christ as we build upon the foundation of Christian ethics.

As we endeavor to live to honor and glorify our Creator, let us seek to live with honesty and integrity toward God, toward others, and toward ourselves.

CHAPTER TWO

A LIFESTYLE OF HONESTY AND INTEGRITY

Who shall ascend into the hill of the LORD? or who shall stand in his holy place? He that hath clean hands, and a pure heart; who hath not lifted up his soul unto vanity, nor sworn deceitfully. He shall receive the blessing from the LORD, and righteousness from the God of his salvation. (Psalm 24:3–5)

He hath shewed thee, O man, what is good; and what doth the LORD require of thee, but to do justly, and to love mercy, and to walk humbly with thy God? (Micah 6:8)

> The just man walketh in his integrity: his children are blessed after him. (Proverbs 20:7)

In William Shakespeare's acclaimed *Hamlet*, the character Polonius gave advice to his son, and his words have become immortalized: "This above all: to thine own self be true." Literary critics disagree among themselves as to the full intent and meaning of these words in *Hamlet*. However, "the modern age has given entirely different meanings to this phrase as it connotes the ideas of truth, self-ownership and individuality" (http://literarydevices.net/to-thine-own-self-be-true/, accessed May 30, 2016). Although we may not know the full intentions of Shakespeare, we know we must be honest with ourselves first if we are to live honestly toward others. We must be real, pure, and sincere with absolute integrity.

No two words better define the essential foundation of ethical conduct than the words honesty and integrity. The essential concepts of these two words represent the core essence of Christian ethics.

Someone has said a person's reputation is what others think he is; his character, however, is what he actually is. Character is what you are in the dark, in times of the most severe testing and in times no one sees you but God. The core of pure ethical conduct is a person living his life with the uncorrupted character of integrity. When integrity is a person's foundation for living, he has discovered the true and essential quality of Christianity. Further, only through the indwelling power of Jesus Christ can one live with the richness of pure integrity.

Honesty and integrity should influence and inform the ethical behavior of an individual in every area of his life.

INTEGRITY IN BUSINESS DEALINGS

We first discover the concept of honesty and integrity in the Old Testament. The concept seems to have originated from the establishment of standards for appropriate and acceptable business practices. Further, God rejected fraudulent behavior and business dealings. Many verses in the Old Testament having to do with integrity or honesty refer to various business instruments and measurements. One of the first instances of such admonitions is in the Book of Leviticus.

> You shall do no injustice in judgment, in measurement of length, weight, or volume. You shall have honest scales, honest weights, an honest ephah, and an honest hin: I am the LORD your God, who brought you out of the land of Egypt. (Leviticus 19:35–36, NKJV)

The Scriptures command the merchant to be unquestionably scrupulous in his business dealings. God clearly condemned dishonest standards of measurement, inaccurate scales and weights, and irregular sales practices. The weights and measurements of a person of integrity must be just and fair, following rigorous, predetermined standards. God detests aberrant business practices that would do any less. Further, God called such dishonesty "unrighteous" and "an abomination." (See Deuteronomy 25:13–16.)

It is interesting that the New International Version translates the word *abomination* with the concept of being "detestable." "For the LORD your God detests anyone who does these things, anyone who deals dishonestly" (Deuteronomy

25:16, NIV). Clearly, God has great disdain for those who take advantage of others to their own selfish and lustful benefit.

There are numerous verses of Scripture throughout the Bible that reveal God's contempt for dishonest practices. Consider, for instance, the following verses: Proverbs 11:1; 12:22; 16:11; 20:10, 23; Ezekiel 45:10; Luke 3:12–13.

The apostle Paul taught we should think of the needs and benefit of others more than we think of our own personal and selfish desires. (See Philippians 2:3–5.) Sadly, it is almost a foreign concept in North American culture with its narcissistic, self-centered focus. We should go the extra mile, going out of our way to ensure our business dealings are fair, just, and honest. That is integrity in God's view.

I well remember a scam that affected many ministers in the 1970s. The scam involved the purchase of luxury automobiles at attractive prices. A number of ministers participated, and while some received their purchased cars, some received lesser vehicles than what they had purchased. Some even received nothing in exchange for their money. It was a pyramid-type scam that ultimately collapsed, hurting numerous people and finally sending the scam artists to prison. God hates deceitful business practices, and He detests individuals taking advantage of others. Such conduct is the perfect picture of unethical behavior, and God hates it.

I once had several rotten fence posts in my backyard fence and I needed to replace them. I had the materials on hand but had not had time to do the work myself. A couple of entrepreneurs knocked on my front door, wanting to do some work on my house. I did not allow them to do the work they were inquiring about, but I quizzed them to see if they would be interested in replacing the fence posts. They accepted the job.

I made the mistake of trusting them and not keeping an eye on their work. When they were finished, everything looked great. Within a few days, however, I discovered they had only cut off and removed the above-ground part of the old posts, cut the new posts to the same above-ground length, and set the new posts in place. They put a small amount of concrete around the base to make them appear to be set in concrete. The only thing holding up the new posts was the existing fence; the posts were supporting nothing. I had to completely remove all of them and soon removed the entire fence. I learned a terribly painful lesson at the hands of crooked entrepreneurs.

God hates dishonesty, cheating, and fraudulent actions. Business dealings should always be completely above board, honest, and fair. Ethics in business dealings is like a two-way street, going both directions. We also should be fair with those who perform services for us. It is unethical to try to squeeze people financially and take advantage of them for our own financial gain. For example, consider ethics in the realm of restaurant service gratuities.

Whether or not a person is a fan of the idea of tipping for restaurant service, that is the system in place and a person should be aware of that before going out to eat. Failing to tip the server despite receiving good service takes advantage of an individual who is only trying to do his or her job and make a living. If we cannot afford to tip or do not plan to tip, we should not eat out. If we eat out and leave no tip, we are essentially defrauding the overworked and underappreciated food server.

Also, consider the impression and testimony you leave behind. If the server knows you claim to be a Christian, what will he or she think of your testimony when you leave them no gratuity? We leave a terrible impression on the world when we selfishly refuse to acknowledge the person's hard work through a fair tip for the service they provide us.

It also is embarrassing to be out with a "Christian" group who mercilessly berates and antagonizes a server over the food, service, or other complaints. Sometimes the group may be loud and obnoxious, generally obstinate and complaining, and depart without leaving even a modest tip. Or sometimes a church group may arrive thirty minutes before closing time and linger, laughing long after the doors are locked. It is inconsiderate conduct.

Pentecostals are easily identified by their appearance, but often we do not know the server. He or she may be the backslid child of a Pentecostal. The server may have been considering visiting our church. We never know who knows us! What kind of testimony is our group leaving behind? What does the server think and feel about us? How does the restaurant management view our group and/or our church? We should consider our testimony among these precious souls.

The fair, ethical, and honest thing to do is to exercise polite and kind manners, be courteous in every transaction, and be considerate of the servers and other patrons within the establishment. Upon leaving, it also is only fair to leave an appropriate gratuity for the services received—even generous, if possible. These ethical actions will leave a positive impression upon both servers and management, and they will reflect fairness, honesty, and integrity.

The concepts of honesty and integrity do not begin and end with one's business dealings and practices. They also extend into every area of a person's relationships.

INTEGRITY IN RELATIONSHIPS

It is commonly known as the Golden Rule: "Do unto others as you would have them do unto you." In fact, many people do not realize the precept is drawn directly from the Holy Bible, but it is: "And as ye would that men should do to you, do ye also to them likewise. . . . But love ye your enemies, and do good, and lend, hoping for nothing again; and your reward shall be great, and ye shall be the children of the Highest: for he is kind unto the unthankful and to the evil" (Luke 6:31–35).

A fundamental, biblical principle reveals we will reap what we sow, and people will treat us in general as we treat them. That is not to suggest we will never be treated unfairly or unkindly as long as we treat others with fairness and kindness. However, if we do treat people with kindness, it certainly will multiply the positive responses we receive from others in turn. And best of all, our conscience and relationship with God will be clear and free from guilt, benefiting us greatly. (See Acts 24:16.)

The people of God should be known as the most honest people with whom one could associate or do business. They should have a flawless reputation of integrity. As Paul wrote to the Christians in Corinth, we should aim to do "what is honorable not only in the Lord's sight but also in the sight of man" (II Corinthians 8:21, ESV). Our conduct should be honest since God sees all we do; however, there is an even higher biblical standard: doing what other people will perceive as being honest. That has to do with our reputation. It is important we have integrity, but it also is important others perceive us to be people of integrity because our conduct reflects on God and His church.

This is one of the reasons Paul, in his epistle to the Romans, indicated they should not let their "good be evil spoken of" (Romans 14:16). He was referring to their reputation with others who might misinterpret their behavior, reflecting negatively on the Lord and His church. The English Standard Version puts it this way: "So do not let what you regard as good be spoken of as evil" (Romans 14:16, ESV).

To the Thessalonians Paul stated, "That ye may walk honestly toward them that are without" (I Thessalonians 4:12). Further, the writer of the Hebrew epistle indicated we ought to be "willing to live honestly" (Hebrews 13:18), which should be the case even when we find ourselves struggling in unfair circumstances. There are no situations in life that justify dishonesty or a breakdown of personal integrity.

INTEGRITY IN UNFAIR CIRCUMSTANCES

Let's face it; sometimes life is not fair. Unfortunate and difficult circumstances come to every person. When a believer finds himself in a difficult season of life, he should continue to live honorably with personal integrity. As difficult as it may be, it is a time for one's true character to manifest through purity and honesty in every area of one's life.

1. Job. Consider Job who went through a season of great trial. Job suffered so greatly his name became synonymous with the idea of suffering: "the suffering of Job." Few individuals have suffered to the extent experienced by Job.

> Job had been lying in unrelieved misery for months with open sores all over his body. During this time he bore the grief of seven dead sons and three dead daughters. All of his wealth had vanished in one

afternoon. He had become repulsive to his wife, loathsome to his brothers, and even little children despised him as he lay on the ash heap outside of town. (John Piper, "Job: The Revelation of God in Suffering," www.desiringgod.org, accessed May 31, 2016)

But through all his sufferings, Job retained his honesty and integrity before God. He refused to succumb to his base, fleshly nature. He maintained his steadfast faith in God and avoided the sting of reproach:

Moreover Job continued his parable, and said, As God liveth, who hath taken away my judgment; and the Almighty, who hath vexed my soul; all the while my breath is in me, and the spirit of God is in my nostrils; my lips shall not speak wickedness, nor my tongue utter deceit. God forbid that I should justify you: till I die I will not remove mine integrity from me. My righteousness I hold fast, and will not let it go: my heart shall not reproach me so long as I live. (Job 27:1–6)

(See also Job 31:1–40.)

The Lord even testified to Satan that Job was perfect, upright, and a man of integrity (Job 2:3).

When the swelling currents of life's challenges come crushing in on us and threaten our survival, our integrity is tried and tested. Time will reveal the strength of our character and the substance of our integrity.

2. Jacob. When Jacob experienced deceit at the hands of his uncle Laban, one cannot feel too sorry for him. After all, Jacob had lived a life of deceit before leaving home. Jacob, whose name meant "supplanter" or "deceiver," had managed to persuade his brother Esau to surrender his birthright in exchange for a bowl of stew. The Hebrew birthright was a legal matter of certain privileges afforded to the firstborn son. Later, executing the plan of his mother, Rebekah, Jacob deceived his dying father into thinking he was Esau and into giving Jacob the blessing. The blessing was another privilege in which the firstborn normally received a greater blessing than the other siblings.

Esau was furious with his brother. Jacob decided it to be in his best interest to leave home, and he fled to his uncle's place. There he worked faithfully for his uncle Laban for many years. Interestingly, it was there Jacob began to reap the bitter harvest of the seeds of deceit he had sown previously.

Jacob agreed to work for Laban for seven years in exchange for receiving Laban's daughter Rachel as his wife. However, upon the wedding night he discovered he had been deceived. Laban had given Jacob his daughter Leah instead of Rachel. Jacob then worked an additional seven years in order to have Rachel for his wife. Further, Laban changed Jacob's wages ten times as Jacob worked for him for a total of about twenty years. (See Genesis 31:1–42.) Surely Jacob was tasting the bitterness of deceit in the same way he had once deceived his own brother, Esau.

Jacob was by this time a changed man and he was experiencing the blessings of God in his life. Perhaps that is one of the reasons God changed his name to Israel following an all-night wrestling match with the angel of the Lord. He had changed from a deceiver to "a prince with God," and God honored him with a new, appropriate name. (See Genesis 32:24–32.) Jacob did not live with character and integrity early in his life, but he demonstrated that it is possible to change one's character. He became a man of integrity who experienced the blessing of God.

3. Joseph. Joseph was one who demonstrated great restraint and personal integrity in his life. He suffered greatly because of the actions of his jealous brothers who sold him into Egyptian slavery. He ended up in the ruler Potiphar's household in Egypt as a highly valued and trusted servant. When approached by Potiphar's wife to have a sexual liaison with her, Joseph flatly refused.

> But he refused, and said unto his master's wife, Behold, my master wotteth not what is with me in the house, and he hath committed all that he hath to my hand; there is none greater in this house than I; neither hath he kept back any thing from me but thee, because thou art his wife: how then can I do this great wickedness, and sin against God? And it came to pass, as she spake to Joseph day by day, that he hearkened not unto her, to lie by her, or to be with her. And it came to pass about this time, that Joseph went into the house to do his business; and there was none of the men of the house there within. And she caught him by his garment, saying, Lie with me: and he left his garment in her hand, and fled, and got him out. (Genesis 39:8–12)

Joseph ended up in prison because of his stand against the advances of Potiphar's wife. He lost his freedom, but he maintained his character and integrity before God. And ultimately—through the sovereign blessing of God—Joseph became the means of saving his entire family from the ravaging famine throughout the entire region.

4. David. Consider the integrity David exhibited when he was running to escape the vindictive hand of King Saul. David and his men had taken shelter in a cave at Engedi. Not knowing David was hiding there, Saul and his men also stopped there for the night. Although some would justify David taking advantage of the opportunity to end the life of Saul and bring closure to his life on the run, David refused to lay a hand on the king. (See I Samuel 24:1–22.) He did, however, quietly use his sword to cut a corner from the king's garment. Even that action caused David to feel remorse and guilt.

> And he said unto his men, The LORD forbid that I should do this thing unto my master, the LORD's anointed, to stretch forth mine hand against him, seeing he is the anointed of the LORD. So David stayed his servants with these words, and suffered them not to rise against Saul. . . . Behold, this day thine eyes have seen how that the LORD had delivered thee to day into mine hand in the cave: and some bade me kill thee: but mine eye spared thee; and I said, I will not put forth mine hand against my lord; for he is the LORD's anointed. . . . Saul said, Is this thy voice, my son David? And Saul lifted up his voice, and wept. And he said to David, Thou art more righteous than I: for thou

hast rewarded me good, whereas I have rewarded thee evil. (I Samuel 24:6–17)

David's integrity would not allow him to touch the anointed of the Lord. He would bide his time and let God be his defender. But even Saul recognized that David was "more righteous" in his godly behavior and integrity than was Saul.

INTEGRITY AS A LIFESTYLE

Integrity and honesty are not one-time actions or elements of behavior that change with the wind. Integrity and honesty are the character foundations of a Christian lifestyle. People either have character or they do not have character. Certainly, a person can change from a lifestyle lacking in honest character to one that is sterling, but for it to be real it must become a genuine lifestyle of committed choice.

Paul testified of his sincere efforts to live with integrity. Notice a couple of his comments in his epistle to the believers in Corinth:

> Therefore seeing we have this ministry, as we have received mercy, we faint not; but have renounced the hidden things of dishonesty, not walking in craftiness, nor handling the word of God deceitfully; but by manifestation of the truth commending ourselves to every man's conscience in the sight of God. (II Corinthians 4:1–2)

> Receive us; we have wronged no man, we have corrupted no man, we have defrauded no man. (II Corinthians 7:2)

An honest lifestyle of integrity requires one to disavow dishonest, crafty, and deceitful practices. Integrity leads him or her to live above reproach and free of corruption or fraudulent conduct. It is a lifestyle that embraces and exalts truth, always endeavoring to live up to the highest standards of transparency and decency.

The prophet Isaiah spoke clearly regarding the blessing in store for those who live with integrity. (See Isaiah 33:15–16.) The New Living Translation presents these two verses with beautiful clarity: "Those who are honest and fair, who refuse to profit by fraud, who stay far away from bribes, who refuse to listen to those who plot murder, who shut their eyes to all enticement to do wrong—these are the ones who will dwell on high. The rocks of the mountains will be their fortress. Food will be supplied to them, and they will have water in abundance" (Isaiah 33:15–16, NLT).

Those who desire blessing in their lives are to live with integrity. They will

- be honest,
- be fair,
- refuse to profit through fraud,
- avoid bribes,
- refuse to listen to evil plots, and
- close their eyes to all enticement to sin.

There are numerous injunctions in the Old Testament that reveal the way of integrity to be the way that is to be pursued by God's people:

- Psalm 24:3–5: Points out the necessity of having "clean hands, and a pure heart," and avoiding vanity and deceitfulness.
- Proverbs 11:3–6: Points toward integrity as being the guide for those who are upright and reveals the destiny of destruction set for the perverse or wicked.
- Proverbs 19:1: Reveals it would be better to be poor and live with integrity than to speak perverseness and be a fool.
- Proverbs 28:6: Further points out it is better to be poor and live with uprightness of character than to be rich materially, but be evil in one's ways.

Jesus Christ pointed out the idea of character in Luke 16:10. Jesus stated, "He that is faithful in that which is least is faithful also in much: and he that is unjust in the least is unjust also in much." In other words, integrity, honesty, and just conduct are either ingrained in one's character or they are sadly lacking from one's character. They are elements that permeate a person's character and flow out from that inward moral fiber, affecting one's actions and conduct.

I was serving as the men's dorm supervisor while teaching at Texas Bible College in Houston in the 1980s. Late one night, a number of students caught a young man trying to steal a car from the campus. Although we never condoned students taking actions to detain or capture would-be criminals on campus, these students did indeed capture the young thief and took him to the prayer room. The prayer room always seemed to me like an appropriate, though ironic, place to take the young man. They detained him there while some students came to my apartment and awakened me. I went down to handle the situation and there saw a boy possibly no older than fifteen or sixteen. The boy was adamantly insisting to the students who had caught him: "I'm a Christian; I'm not a sinner. You just caught me committing a sin." His lack of character and integrity did not just cause the boy to "commit a sin." It created in him a flaw that informed his overall behavior, contrary to his supposed Christian testimony.

Ethics is not complicated. It is a matter of doing what one knows to be right, pure, and honest. Usually we know immediately what the right course of action is; we have to determine to make the right decision and do what is right. In order to prepare our heart always to respond with integrity, the believer should follow the advice of Paul in his epistle to the Philippians—to think on good and pure things:

> Finally, brethren, whatsoever things are true, whatsoever things are honest, whatsoever things are just, whatsoever things are pure, whatsoever things are lovely, whatsoever things are of good report; if there be any virtue, and if there be any praise, think on these things. (Philippians 4:8)

If we will set our affections on heavenly things—things holy, righteous, and pure—we will position ourselves to walk in righteousness with honesty and integrity in everything we do.

At the root of ethical behavior is a lifestyle of integrity. Integrity flows into a person's conduct and informs that person's decisions on ethical choices. Integrity is intimately connected to sincerity. One might think, *Oh, but one can be sincere and be sincerely wrong.* That is true on a certain level, but it misses the core meaning of the word *sincere*.

The word *sincerity* in the Old Testament is translated from the Hebrew word *tāmîm*, which means "complete, sound . . . whole, entire. . . sound, healthful. . . . wholesome, unimpaired, innocent, having integrity. . . . what is complete, entirely in accord with truth and fact" (Francis Brown, Samuel Rolles Driver, and Charles Augustus Briggs, *Enhanced Brown-Driver-Briggs Hebrew and English Lexicon* [Oxford: Clarendon Press, 1977], 1071).

According to ancient folklore, some merchants used wax to fill in and cover defects in pottery. On hot days the wax supposedly would melt, revealing the imperfect condition of the vase and disappointing the owner. This folklore indicated that quality, perfect products were labeled with the term *sine cera*, which meant "without wax," to indicate the guaranteed quality of the product. Whether true or not, the premise remains true: That which is sincere is complete, whole, and entire— having integrity. Integrity indicates completeness, and in that complete state it conveys the idea of strength and durability.

We are to be sincere, but beyond that we are to possess absolute integrity in our character and lifestyle. We should always seek to be honest, forthright, and holy in all our ways and conduct.

CHAPTER THREE

A LIFESTYLE OF LOYALTY

Be ye followers of me, even as I also am of Christ.
(I Corinthians 11:1)

(See also I Corinthians 4:16; Ephesians 5:1;
Philippians 3:17.)

In this chapter we will consider three basic topics: (1) what is loyalty; (2) to whom do we owe loyalty; and (3) loyalty, how far. Further, as was the case with integrity, we will discover and explore how loyalty should become a faithful lifestyle for believers.

WHAT IS LOYALTY?

Loyalty has to do with steadfastness, faithfulness, and allegiance.

Merriam-Webster Dictionary defines *loyal* as "unswerving in allegiance: as a : faithful in allegiance to one's lawful sovereign or government b : faithful to a private person to whom fidelity is due c : faithful to a cause, ideal, custom, institution, or product."

Clearly, believers should be unswervingly faithful in their allegiance to Jesus Christ. Also, believers should have a limited sense of allegiance to government, fellow citizens and believers, and to certain ideals and institutions. Believers should subordinate their allegiance in everything to their overarching loyalty to Jesus Christ and His church. We should let no one try to persuade us of any obligation to be loyal to anything or anyone that is in conflict with our loyalty to Jesus Christ. The Sovereign of this universe is supreme and above all. Our loyalty in every area of life must hinge upon our primary obligation to Him and His Word.

Loyalty is a wonderful trait that is too often in rare supply in our world. For example, in recent years individuals spent their entire career working at one company. Their long-term employment exhibited both their loyalty toward the company and the company's loyalty toward them. Today, that is more often not the case. Many employees are sacrificed with little forethought by the company in order to improve the stockholders' dividends. There is extremely little loyalty toward long-term employees, and consequently, loyalty is rare among employees toward their employers. Each entity is looking exclusively at the bottom line: "What's best for me?" or "What's best for the company?"

When a person or company does encounter a rare individual of intense loyalty, it is usually noticed and appreciated. It is like discovering a rare gem of exquisite quality to be appreciated, valued, and guarded.

What examples of loyalty could we discover in the Scriptures? While loyalty is not a prominent scriptural topic, its companion topic of faithfulness is.

David and Jonathan. Perhaps one of the most notable examples of loyalty in the Bible is the story of David and Jonathan. Theirs was a friendship so strong the loyalty between them was striking.

As the son of King Saul, Jonathan was heir to the throne of Israel in the days prior to the divided kingdom. Despite this, Jonathan believed in David and supported his anointing as the future king. However, because of Saul's immense jealousy toward David, there was great pressure exerted against their friendship. Still, none of the barriers to their friendship destroyed Jonathan's loyalty toward David.

> And it came to pass, when he had made an end of speaking unto Saul, that the soul of Jonathan was knit with the soul of David, and Jonathan loved him as his own soul. And Saul took him that day, and would let him go no more home to his father's house. Then Jonathan and David made a covenant, because he loved him as his own soul. And Jonathan stripped himself of the robe that was upon him, and gave it to David. (I Samuel 18:1–4)

In a world where loyalty often is nonexistent, the kind of loyalty Jonathan showed toward his friend David is notable. Jonathan was the blood-heir to the throne; he could have become king. But Jonathan possessed a quality in his character and spirit that transcended the power of being king over an earthly kingdom. Jonathan was unswervingly faithful to his friend David with absolute loyalty.

There were days when Saul in his jealous rage was determined to find and kill David. Often, however, Jonathan would quietly send word of warning to David in an effort to protect him. Jonathan intervened in many ways on David's behalf. (See I Samuel 19:1–5; 23:16.) Jonathan was loyal to David unto death even though his father Saul continued to oppose David and seek to kill him.

When David received word of Saul's and Jonathan's deaths in battle, he wept and mourned the loss. As Jonathan was loyal to David, so David was loyal to his friend Jonathan. In his mourning, David penned beautiful words that reflected his loyalty. "I am distressed for thee, my brother Jonathan: very pleasant hast thou been unto me: thy love to me was wonderful, passing the love of women" (II Samuel 1:26).

It is unfortunate some individuals in our perverted and evil culture desire to frame David and Jonathan's loyal relationship with twisted sexual overtones. Theirs was a pure love, not one of sexual lust and perversion. Their mutual love was a rare example of faithfulness in its purest form.

Further, it was a measure of loyalty that transcended death. David later sought out and honored Mephibosheth, the lame son of Jonathan. He brought Mephibosheth to live at the palace and eat at his own table. This he did in honor of his friend Jonathan.

And David said, Is there yet any that is left of the house of Saul, that I may shew him kindness for Jonathan's sake? . . . Jonathan hath yet a son, which is lame on his feet. . . . Now when Mephibosheth, the son of Jonathan, the son of Saul, was come unto David, he fell on his face, and did reverence. And David said, Mephibosheth. . . . Fear not: for I will surely shew thee kindness for Jonathan thy father's sake, and will restore thee all the land of Saul thy father; and thou shalt eat bread at my table continually. (II Samuel 9:1–7)

Ruth. Ruth's loyalty to her mother-in-law, Naomi, is another beautiful story in Scripture of faithfulness. Naomi and her family had moved to Moab to seek relief from the raging famine in Bethlehem. There in a foreign land her husband Elimelech died, and her two sons, Mahlon and Chilion, took wives who were Moabites. Some ten years later her sons also died, leaving Naomi and her two Moabitess daughters-in-law to mourn their deaths.

Naomi had lost everything in Moab. She was determined to return to her homeland in Bethlehem. Ruth and Orpah, her daughters-in-law, were inclined to go with her, but Naomi discouraged them from going. She knew it would be to them a foreign land with strange customs and an unfamiliar religion. (See Ruth 1:12–15.) Orpah returned home, but Ruth was insistent. Her response to Naomi has become a timeless anthem of loyalty.

> And Ruth said, Entreat me not to leave thee, or to return from following after thee: for whither thou goest, I will go; and where thou lodgest, I will lodge: thy people shall be my people, and thy God my God: where thou diest, will I die, and there will I be buried: the LORD do so to me, and more also, if ought but death part thee and me. (Ruth 1:16–17)

Ruth's unfailing loyalty toward Naomi formed the foundation for one of the greatest love stories ever told. The rest of the Book of Ruth goes on to detail their journey to Bethlehem and their settling into a new life. There Ruth discovered a happy future in a new land with a new life. A man named Boaz (a wealthy relative to Elimelech) made overtures toward Ruth, and eventually fulfilled the role of near-kinsman redeemer. He married Ruth and brought this Moabitess into the lineage of the future King of kings and Lord of lords, the Son of God. What a picture of God's grace, and what a picture of loyalty!

Joab. Another Old Testament story of loyalty appears in the story of Joab's faithfulness to David. *The Lexham Bible Dictionary* makes note of the following points of Joab's loyalty:

- (II Samuel 3:24–25): "His accusation that Abner was spying is based on loyalty."
- (II Samuel 12:26–28): "He refused to complete the victory against the Ammonites so that David would claim the credit for it."
- (II Samuel 18:2): "He was loyal to David during Absalom's coup" (Edward J. Bridge, "Joab the Commander," ed. John D. Barry et al., *The Lexham Bible Dictionary*

[Bellingham, WA: Lexham Press, 2012, 2013, 2014, 2015]).

Loyalty, as defined in the *Dictionary of Bible Themes*, is "A commitment to an ongoing relationship and to the attitude and behaviour demanded by it. It is evident in human relationships and also in the covenant relationship between God and his people" (Martin H. Manser, *Dictionary of Bible Themes: The Accessible and Comprehensive Tool for Topical Studies* [London: Martin Manser, 2009]).

TO WHOM DO WE OWE LOYALTY?

In the Scriptures we see loyalty exhibited by God toward His people and through His covenants and promises. We also see the loyalty of God's people toward Him, although His people often wavered and failed to maintain their faithfulness. Finally, we also witness loyalty in human relationships among family and friends and toward those in authority.

Believers should be a strongly loyal people—first to God, but then also to others. There are various levels of responsibility and accountability, but we should exhibit loyalty on every level. Believers should meet their biblical obligations and be known as a trustworthy people of faith. To adequately assess and understand wherein our loyalties should rest, it is vital to build our understanding of loyalty on the right foundation. Our loyalty is first and primarily to God. We must first get the foundation right; then we can proceed to understand loyalty.

LOYALTY TO JESUS CHRIST

If we owe anyone or anything unswerving faithfulness, it is the One who gave His life to redeem us from sin. To Him we owe our all; to Him we owe absolute loyalty in everything.

In I Thessalonians 1, Paul wrote of the Thessalonian believers' "work of faith, and labour of love, and patience of hope in our Lord Jesus Christ" (I Thessalonians 1:3). He further praised their loyalty toward God and toward himself as their leader: "As ye know what manner of men we were among you for your sake. And ye became followers of us, and of the Lord, having received the word in much affliction, with joy of the Holy Ghost: so that ye were ensamples to all that believe in Macedonia and Achaia" (I Thessalonians 1:5–7). He could praise their loyalty to himself only because (1) he was loyal to God and (2) they were loyal to God. Without loyalty to the Lord, our loyalty toward our fellow man is shallow and lacks eternal significance.

The writer of the Hebrew epistle encouraged believers, "Let us hold fast the confession of our hope without wavering, for he who promised is faithful" (Hebrews 10:23, ESV). God is loyal—unswervingly faithful—to us, so we should be loyal to Him and to His gospel. We are debtors to Jesus Christ and owe Him our complete loyalty. (See Romans 12:1–2.)

There is absolutely nothing we can do to deserve or merit salvation in Christ Jesus. We cannot purchase or earn our salvation. Redemption is the free gift of Jesus Christ to those who positively respond to His call and receive His redemptive provision. However, the redemptive work of Jesus Christ in us will bear fruit in our lives, which will manifest through good works. "For by grace are ye saved through faith; and that not of yourselves: it is the gift of God: not of works, lest any man should boast. For we are his workmanship, created in Christ Jesus unto good works, which God hath before ordained that we should walk in them" (Ephesians 2:8–10). The salvation Christ has wrought in our lives will cause our "good works" to reflect intense loyalty and faithfulness to the Lord.

We do not produce good works to buy salvation, for it is beyond purchase. But we do endeavor to demonstrate our loyalty to Christ through our faithful adherence to Him and to His Word. Part of our faithfulness and loyalty to Christ involves our faithfulness and loyalty to authorities, friends, and family. However, we should clearly understand the parameters of loyalty and know its limitations.

LIMITATIONS OF LOYALTY

Are there any limitations to loyalty? Is biblical loyalty to be unswerving devotion to another person regardless of that person's actions, behavior, or ideals?

This is a day and culture in which it is vital to understand the limitations and boundaries of loyalty. For example, sexual immorality is a cancerous evil of our society that places definite limitations on loyalty. Loyalty is commendable, but when a child faces a sexual affront by a trusted friend or loved one, loyalty is dismissed. That child owes absolutely no loyalty to anyone who would attempt to violate him or her sexually. Even the bond of parental authority is broken when a parent attempts to violate one of his or her children sexually or physically. Abuse breaks the bond of loyalty.

The Roman Catholic Church has suffered terrible scandal over the last several decades because of sexual abuses in the church. Children were violated by authority figures of the church, and then the church shielded and protected the aggressors rather than the children. This illustrates clearly one of the boundaries or limits of loyalty. We owe no loyalty to authority figures who would abuse us verbally, physically, spiritually, or sexually.

The Scriptures teach, "Children, obey your parents in the Lord: for this is right" (Ephesians 6:1). It is no accident Paul said "in the Lord." When parents are not serving the Lord it frees the children to some degree from their responsibilities to parental authority. The biblical perspective of this position is evident in the disciples' response to the authorities in Acts 4 and Acts 5:

> And they called them, and commanded them not to speak at all nor teach in the name of Jesus. But Peter and John answered and said unto them, Whether it be right in the sight of God to hearken unto you more than unto God, judge ye. (Acts 4:18–19)

> Then Peter and the other apostles answered and said, We ought to obey God rather than men. (Acts 5:29)

Loyalty is closely associated with several key biblical concepts: authority, obedience, unity, fellowship, leadership, submission, and subjection, to name only several. These biblical themes are vital, but a Christian's obligation to each is tempered and balanced by his or her supreme responsibilities to God.

Our loyalty is to God first and foremost. When any other relationship detracts from that primary duty toward God, we are released from obligations of loyalty.

There is no virtue solely in authority, obedience, unity, or submission in and of themselves. For example, it is no virtue for one to obey someone in authority who orders that person to do anything contrary to the Scriptures. What benefit is there in unity if those unified are united in rebellion or in unbiblical practices? Individuals can unite themselves in crime or other sins. Submission to those who would lead us into iniquity has no virtue whatsoever. So, the virtue then is not in authority, obedience, unity, or submission. The virtue of these is in the greater noble cause to which they join us. Absent that noble cause, there is no virtue.

There is no authority or power on earth that is higher than God's. Therefore, every aspect of human authority must be subordinate to the loyalty we are to give to God's authority. (See Romans 13:1–8.)

We are to be committed to the "*higher* powers" (Romans 13:1). What are the higher powers? The higher powers are the structures of authority as designed and created by God. As long as authoritarian structures remain rooted in biblically sound principles, they carry the ordination and approval of God. When they leave those principles and lead others away from godly fundamentals instead of toward them, they lose God's blessing. For example, governmental authority has the sanction of God to achieve law, order, and civility in society. But our obligations to government, to authority, and to other human beings have limits.

Perhaps Paul best expressed our responsibility of loyalty when he wrote, "Be ye followers of me, even as I also am of Christ" (I Corinthians 11:1). We are to observe authority and follow human leaders only as long as they follow Jesus Christ. At a minimum, they must not violate our relationship with Christ or lead contrary to His Word. Our supreme call and responsibility is to follow Jesus Christ and be loyal to Him.

When something or someone does not lead us in the paths of the Lord Jesus Christ, we are free from the authority spiritually, if not legally.

Consider the story of Jim Jones and his followers and their tragic end in Jonestown, Guyana. On November 18, 1978, Jones led his followers in a great human massacre. More than nine hundred followers died in a mass murder-suicide as they loyally followed the direction of their delusional, cultic leader. The people had followed Jones from Indiana to California to Guyana. On that fateful day, Jones led his followers to drink poisonous Kool-Aid. They had followed him by choice, but in the end Jones utilized armed guards to ensure the people followed his suicidal orders. Loyalty has its limits.

LOYALTY AS A LIFESTYLE

Christians should be loyal, dependable people. Others should feel confident in sharing with them confidential matters, knowing they will not betray the trust placed in them. They should be able to have confidence a Christian will do his or her best to help them and pray with them. People deserve to know Christians will not run to others revealing problems shared in confidence, spreading gossip like uncontrolled wildfire.

When a person lives his or her life in a dependable fashion, others will come to trust the person. Trust and dependability are part of the foundation of loyalty—both to the one who gives loyalty and to the recipient. Trustworthiness and dependability exhibit loyalty, but they also earn loyalty from others. Trustworthiness and dependability engender loyalty.

I am well acquainted with a gentleman who was once accused of being disloyal because he dared to stand on principle in opposition to his accuser. Perhaps he made errors of judgment in how he went about dealing with their disagreement. However, he was right to stand on biblical and conscientious principle even though it conflicted with the opinion of another individual.

When we have differences of opinion, we should endeavor to work through those differences as Christians. Name-calling or impugning the character of those with whom we disagree is unethical. In I Peter 5:2–3 a principle is directed toward pastors, but the principle extends beyond pastors.

> Feed the flock of God which is among you, taking the oversight thereof, not by constraint, but willingly; not for filthy lucre, but of a ready mind; neither as being lords over God's heritage, but being ensamples to the flock. (I Peter 5:2–3)

Those who serve in Christian leadership positions should lead as humble servants. Further, they should lead by example, not by coercive authoritarianism. As pastors are instructed not to act as "lords over God's heritage," neither should any leader lead from an elitist, superior, authoritarian attitude. In the church we are all believers—all children of our heavenly Father. We all have different positions, responsibilities, and places in the body of Jesus Christ, so we function accordingly within the body. However, Paul taught us to submit one to another in the fear of God (Ephesians 5:21).

Jesus Christ was loyal to us; we have a responsibility to be loyal to Him. In the same sense, leaders and followers within the body of Christ are to be mutually loyal to each other. They are to submit in love to one another for the sake of leading Christ's church. Attitudes that dismiss others or relegate them to a status of unimportance or inferiority have no place in the body of Christ. Every member of the body is significant and has a vital role to play. All should fulfill their roles with diligence and love for others, exercising their responsibilities with mutual loyalty.

CHAPTER FOUR

THE SACREDNESS OF TRUST AND CONFIDENCE

For the which cause I also suffer these things: nevertheless I am not ashamed: for I know whom I have believed, and am persuaded that he is able to keep that which I have committed unto him against that day. (II Timothy 1:12)

How wonderful to know the Lord is fully capable of keeping that which we have committed to Him against the future Day of Judgment! He is trustworthy and He keeps our confidences securely in His divine love and care.

Imagine you have shared your most intimate secret with your best friend. In a moment of severe stress and loneliness you felt you had to talk to someone. With whom could you hope to bare your soul more than with your closest friend on earth?

What a privilege to be able to share confidence with a trusted friend!

Now suppose several days have passed and through a third party you discover your secret is no longer a secret at all. Evidently, your trusted friend has broken confidence and spilled your entire privacy out for the consumption of greedy ears. What a change in your feelings now!

Your most trusted and dear friend suddenly becomes a repugnant object of great disdain. Your feelings of privilege to have a confidant have turned to a sense of angry betrayal. You are disillusioned, dejected, angry, and hurt. You have reaped the bitter harvest of broken trust.

> Confidence in an unfaithful man in time of trouble
> is like a broken tooth, and a foot out of joint.
> (Proverbs 25:19)

THE VALUE OF CONFIDENCE

There is tremendous human value in having close friends with whom we can share a sacred confidence. Such confidence is born out of a high level of trust and respect. Trust is the deepest level of faith. We say we have "faith" in God, but do we "trust" Him when things are going contrary to our desires? Trust is faith, but trust is the deepest possible dimension of faith. We can have faith in God, but when we have lost our dearest loved one to death, we desperately need trust to become active. We need trust to carry us when we can hardly carry ourselves.

There is no higher, greater object of our faith and trust than Jesus Christ. We have staked our trust in Him for the redemption of our eternal soul. We lean upon Him in times of distress, hurt, and disappointment. He is the Rock who never moves, who is forever and always the same—dependable and faithful. As Paul suggested, I know the One in whom I have believed and placed all my trust. I am convinced He is able to keep secure all I have committed into His hands. (See II Timothy 1:12.)

There is great value in having trusted friends in whom we can place our confidence, but humans are fragile, weak, and fallible. God alone never fails.

> It is better to trust in the LORD than to put confidence in man. It is better to trust in the LORD than to put confidence in princes. (Psalm 118:8–9)

> For the LORD shall be thy confidence, and shall keep thy foot from being taken. (Proverbs 3:26)

> In the fear of the LORD is strong confidence: and his children shall have a place of refuge. The fear of the LORD is a fountain of life, to depart from the snares of death. (Proverbs 14:26–27)

First and foremost, we should place and keep our confidence in Jesus Christ. Through our relationship with Christ and His church, however, we will develop other friends in whom we also will place confidence. We must temper the confidence we place in fellow believers with the realistic knowledge of their human frame. We need to continually recognize their frailty as humans, for only the Lord is unfailingly faithful. Still, trusted human friends are invaluable.

We all need friends on whom we can sometimes lean for strength, ones to whom we can turn for prayer, advice, and compassion. There are times when we need to know someone cares enough to listen, to love, and to pray. What a sacred trust when someone turns to us for help! What a great responsibility when someone shares a confidence with us!

KEEPING CONFIDENCE

Paul expressed great confidence in the Corinthian believers. He wrote, "I rejoice therefore that I have confidence in you in all things" (II Corinthians 7:16). It is wonderful to have the trust of another, and it is also a great responsibility.

It is a great duty to share another person's confidence. When that person trusts us and asks us to keep a matter confidential, it is a matter of great duty. We become partaker in one of the highest possible levels of relationship. It is a sacred level of friendship into which we should never enter lightly or regard casually.

Consider the contrast between the loyalty that exists between two committed friends and the basic loyalty toward humanity exhibited by the good Samaritan. A man fell victim to thieves on the treacherous road between Jerusalem and Jericho. Although a priest and a Levite both passed him by with little regard, a Samaritan stopped and rendered aid to the man. He took the wounded man to an inn and paid for his lodging, pledging to pay any extra expense incurred upon his return. (See chapter 1 under "Created to Serve.")

The Samaritan did not know the wounded traveler. He owed the man nothing based on loyalty of friendship because they were not friends. He had made no pledge or commitment to the wounded traveler. Still, he had a sense of loyalty to the common responsibility we share with all our fellow man. He became involved and went out of his way to help the wounded.

With a shared confidence, however, we knowingly accept and make a sacred commitment of trust with the confidant. By allowing that person to share a confidence with us, we become caretaker to that shared trust. It is a holy obligation we have taken on; it is a sacred trust and duty of honor. What a heavy responsibility we have in such a situation! How could we dare betray that person's trust placed in us? Yet some people—even Christians—are terribly sloppy and careless with information that was shared with them in confidence. But breaking confidence also breaks and irreparably damages the trust between two individuals.

I once was aware of two men having breakfast together. As they enjoyed their meal, they talked about many things of mutual interest. At some point in their conversation, however, one of them began sharing information that would have been shared only in the strictest confidence. At a later date after the two had shared that meal, the one man mentioned to me the circumstances of their time together. He added, "I would never share anything with him in confidence—anything that I didn't want the world to know." His trust and respect for the other gentleman had been completely shattered, for someone's sacred trust had been broken.

Faithfully keeping a person's trust and confidence is a high matter of ethics. What the man did in breaking the confidence of another was an act of great betrayal and unfaithfulness. It represented a severe departure from ethical conduct. He broke the trust of another individual.

BROKEN TRUST

Did you ever break the trust your parents had placed in you? Perhaps they trusted you to go to a certain place, but instead you went somewhere you knew would meet their disapproval. Sometime later they found out what had transpired, and they experienced a crestfallen sense of broken trust. It is akin to the same emotions you experience when your confidence is broken by another individual and you feel betrayed. You can imagine why it took time for your relationship of trust and respect with your parents to heal.

It is a serious infringement upon common human decency to betray the confidence of someone who has entrusted us with confidential information. Little wonder murders rage in the city streets and wars are waged around the globe when one realizes the shortage of respect for others.

A particular joke is sometimes told of three participants of various religious faiths. It has been told with many variations, and only in good humor, but the joke does make a poignant point. Three individuals decide to share their greatest weakness or sin in confidence to the others. After two of them have confessed their sinful weakness to the others, the third participant reveals that his weakness is gossip. He can hardly wait to get back to share his newly discovered information with others!

While the joke brings a chuckle, it is often frighteningly too close to the truth. Far too many professing Christians of various stripes find enjoyment in participating in gossip. Some Christians often will try to disguise the gossip as a prayer request, but the motivation usually appears all too clear. It is unfortunate when a Christian cannot be trusted to keep the sacred trust and confidence of a fellow believer.

To gossip is one of the cruelest sins. Its seeds spread into the four winds like a seeded dandelion blown into the light spring air. Everywhere the seeds of gossip fall they do indescribable damage. They damage the reputation of the one spoken against and also to the human relationships of all involved. Imagine the unmitigated pain and hurts caused through cheap gossip!

SACRED TRUST

Trust is sacred, especially when shared with others in confidence. Something that is sacred is also holy. We ought to be careful how we handle holy things, and that certainly should include how we handle the sacred trust others place in us. God is concerned with how we handle "holy things."

Ezekiel 44:8 may appear to some individuals as outdated, disconnected information about the Old Testament Temple and the functions of the Law. But the verse opens a small window of insight into God's serious perspective concerning that which He has deemed to be holy: "And ye have not kept the charge of mine holy things: but ye have set keepers of my charge in my sanctuary for yourselves." With God, holy things are to be guarded and handled with the utmost care.

Keeping the sacred trust of another person is a holy commitment. We must take seriously all of our commitments, and especially those we make to individuals who depend on us to keep their confidence and trust unbroken. Only then will we discover the purity of the highest dimension of sacred trust. We will be the kind of friend everyone wants to have, and we will have many friends. Others will trust and respect us—two of the surest foundations of intimate friendship.

It is important to have the confidence of others, but there is One whose trust and confidence in us is even more important.

GOD'S CONFIDENCE IN US

It is important for our friends to trust us, but how much more important it is for God to have confidence in us! When God allows us to walk through valleys of temptation and testing, He is expressing His level of confidence and trust in us. God promised through Paul He would put no more upon us than we are able to bear (I Corinthians 10:13). He further promised to provide a way of escape. In times of testing, God is saying, "My child, I have confidence in you. You can walk through this valley and come out victorious and stronger in the final analysis."

God has placed much confidence in His people as members of His body on earth. He has given us a calling and a task for ministry to a lost world. We need to be faithful believers, keeping that which He has entrusted to our care. Among those things with which He has entrusted us is the sacred responsibility toward our brothers and sisters in Christ. We should be the trusted friends and confidants our fellow believers need. When they place their confidence in us, we must not let them down and disappoint them through unethical behavior. We have a responsibility of trust.

If we are to grow in trustworthiness beyond our current responsibilities, we must first demonstrate faithfulness in what has already been entrusted to us. Jesus said, "One who is faithful in a very little is also faithful in much, and one who is dishonest in a very little is also dishonest in much. If then you have not been faithful in the unrighteous wealth, who will entrust to you the true riches? And if you have not been faithful in that which is another's, who will give you that which is your own?" (Luke 16:10–12, ESV).

CHAPTER FIVE

ETHICS IN HORIZONTAL RELATIONSHIPS

If it be possible, as much as lieth in you, live peaceably with all men. (Romans 12:18)

Follow peace with all men, and holiness, without which no man shall see the Lord. (Hebrews 12:14)

We began this study by laying out several foundational chapters that contain some of the most vital principles for understanding what ethical conduct is. As we build upon that foundation, we will look out to a world of individuals with whom we interact and deal on a daily basis. What are some general governing ethics for relationships with people? In this chapter we will begin to examine the broader realm of Christian ethics.

What does it take for two people to get along? Perhaps the answer rests in childhood. Can you remember back to your childhood when another toddler wanted the toy you had picked up? The other child had no interest in that toy until you picked it up, but suddenly it became the most popular toy in the room. Or possibly the scenario played out in reverse because we all were born with a self-centered human nature. Self-centeredness is a characteristic we must conquer and control if we are to get along with others.

Shortly before my wife and I were married a dear minister friend wisely counseled me about marriage. Flying in the face of the timeless idea marriage is a 50/50 proposition, he banished the whole idea. "No," he said. "It's more like 70/30! Sometimes you're 70; sometimes you're 30." In other words, a successful marriage necessarily involves continual give-and-take by both husband and wife. It requires two mature adults recognizing that neither will get his or her way all the time. It requires the two release their selfish ambitions in interest of a relationship beneficial to both.

Paul said it this way to the believers in Philippi: "Do nothing from selfish ambition or conceit, but in humility count others more significant than yourselves. Let each of you look not only to his own interests, but also to the interests of others" (Philippians 2:3–4, ESV). Paul went on to exhort them to have the mind of Christ Jesus. For our redemption, Christ set aside His reputation and became a servant, humbling Himself and dying on the cross for our salvation (Philippians 2:5–11). What an example Christ set before us!

Being considerate of the needs, thoughts, opinions, and desires of others is the real key to successful relationships. Patience, kindness, understanding, tolerance, and love are some of the Christian qualities that empower a person to enjoy smooth relationships with his or her peers. All these are vital to establishing a code of ethical conduct toward our fellow man.

HORIZONTAL VERSUS VERTICAL RELATIONSHIPS

What do we mean by "horizontal" relationships? Horizontal relationships refer to those we maintain with our peers, as opposed to "vertical" relationships. Vertical relationships are those we maintain with those in authority over us, or those who are under our authority by virtue of position or delegated responsibilities. Treating others with kindness and consideration enables us to enjoy mutually beneficial and pleasant relationships that reflect the highest and purest qualities of Christian ethics.

While many of the principles of ethical conduct are identical, in this chapter we look primarily at horizontal relationships—those with our peers.

THE GOLDEN RULE

Mentioned earlier in this book, the Golden Rule is vital to all ethical behavior. Jesus was candid and clear in His assessment: "Therefore all things whatsoever ye would that men should do to you, do ye even so to them: for this is the law and the prophets" (Matthew 7:12). (See also Luke 6:31.) One of the highest principles of Christian ethics is treating others as we would want to be treated; it is that simple. If you would not appreciate being treated a certain way, why would you even consider treating someone else in that fashion? Treat others right and it will come back to you.

Humility will lead a person to think less of himself and more of the needs and concerns of others. The prophet Micah succinctly expressed the Lord's view of the fundamental essence of ethical conduct when he prophetically spoke, "He hath shewed thee, O man, what is good; and what doth the LORD require of thee, but to do justly, and to love mercy, and to walk humbly with thy God?" (Micah 6:8). Is that not the crux of the whole matter of living a good life and enjoying profitable relationships with others? To enjoy good relationships with our peers, we should observe the Golden Rule, do what is right, extend mercy, and walk humbly with God. It is not difficult to understand, but neither is it easy to put into practice.

Romans 12 presents several outstanding principles the believer should pursue. They will support one's effort to live with ethical purity toward other people. Paul first urged the Romans to present themselves as living sacrifices, not continually thinking of their own selfish egos, needs, and desires (verses 1–2). Paul then admonished them not to think more highly of themselves than they ought to think (verse 3). Paul was trying to move them away from self-centeredness toward humility. Christians should live sacrificially for Christ and for the body of Christ, the church. (See Romans 12:4–8.)

For the rest of Romans 12, Paul mentioned numerous principles and characteristics we all should strive to attain. If we follow these, we will discover a number of excellent keys to ethical conduct among our peers.

> Nowhere else in Paul's writings do we find a more concise collection of ethical injunctions. In these five verses are thirteen exhortations ranging from love of Christians to hospitality for strangers. There are no finite verbs in the paragraph. There are, however, ten participles that serve as

imperatives. In the three other clauses (vv. 9, 10, 11) an imperative must be supplied. Each of the thirteen exhortations could serve as the text for a full-length sermon. What they deal with are basic to effective Christian living. (Robert H. Mounce, Romans, vol. 27, The New American Commentary [Nashville: Broadman & Holman Publishers, 1995], 236)

Be Real—No Hypocrisy

First of all, we need to be real—sincere, honest, pure-hearted, and without hypocrisy. "Let love be without hypocrisy. Abhor what is evil. Cling to what is good" (Romans 12:9, NKJV). People are weary of fake individuals who put on a good façade but who are not genuine; they are hypocrites.

Often in many downtown areas of smaller communities one can observe what is known as façades. A façade is a false front. We often encounter these in older towns where the buildings also are old. Sometimes the community or local businesses will build façades along the front of the rooftops, giving the buildings a more modern and uniform appearance. Should one visit the rooftops, however, he will observe what is behind the façades: typically, two-by-fours bracing and holding the façade from behind. They are not real; they are only fake fronts. And sadly, there are many people like that. Their front exterior looks nice, but there is no substance behind their façade.

The first and most important principle for maintaining Christian ethics is that we be genuine Christians. The word "Christian" suggests one is a follower of Christ, and Christlike. Belonging to a church congregation does not make us Christians. Patterning our lives after the model of Jesus Christ and experiencing the salvation He has provided is what makes us Christians. We must be real, genuine, and sincere, for others can detect our hypocrisy if we are a fraud.

Theodore Roosevelt is believed to have popularized the saying, "Nobody cares how much you know until they know how much you care" (www.theodorerooseveltcenter.org, accessed June 8, 2016). People want to know you genuinely care about them, and that your care for them is real and not a sham of hypocrisy.

Prefer One Another with Kind Affection

If we are genuine in our relationship with Jesus Christ, we will endeavor to treat others with kindness and affection. Paul wrote, "Be kindly affectioned one to another with brotherly love; in honour preferring one another" (Romans 12:10). We are quick to assess "What's in it for me?" and slow to evaluate what might be the needs and concerns of others. That is human nature; perhaps it flows out of the basic survival instinct with which God has endowed us all.

As Christians we are to have a new nature that rises above the base human nature. It is a nature that genuinely cares about others—even giving others preference over our own selfish ambitions. (See Leviticus 19:18; I Corinthians 10:24; 13:5.) Bearing with and ministering to the weaknesses and needs of others produces harmony in our relationships.

> We who are strong have an obligation to bear with the failings of the weak, and not to please ourselves. Let each of us please his neighbor for his good, to build him up. For Christ did not

please himself, but as it is written, 'The reproaches of those who reproached you fell on me.' For whatever was written in former days was written for our instruction, that through endurance and through the encouragement of the Scriptures we might have hope. May the God of endurance and encouragement grant you to live in such harmony with one another, in accord with Christ Jesus. (Romans 15:1–5, ESV)

Be Diligent and Fervent
When it comes to conducting business or developing healthy relationships, diligence and fervency will cultivate respect among those with whom we associate. People dislike trying to deal with individuals who are slothful, sloppy, and lackadaisical in their business practices or attitudes. If anything is worth doing, it is worth doing right. There is no excuse for lethargy and carelessness when it comes to conducting business or developing ethical relationships.

I knew a man who wore a self-winding watch. The watch wound itself through the movement of the man's body. His boss playfully accused him of being the only one he knew whose self-winding watch would run down. He was teasing the man in good nature, but the point to be learned is clear. We should be diligent and busy about our work.

Be Patient
An entire book could be written on the need for showing patience in our relationships with others. Some people may try our soul and sanity, but patience will help us to deal with

them kindly. When we are tempted to lose our patience with others, we should remember how Christ has dealt with us. Jesus Christ exhibited much patience in all His dealings with humankind. Further, Christ continues to love us and extend exceedingly great patience to us.

What right have we to be short and impatient with others when we consider the grace of Jesus Christ that has benefited us? Paul wrote to the Corinthians regarding love, and among the greatest characteristics of love he mentioned were patience and kindness. "Love is patient and kind; love does not envy or boast; it is not arrogant or rude. It does not insist on its own way; it is not irritable or resentful" (I Corinthians 13:4-5, ESV).

Patience will help us in our pursuit of Christian ethics. When we are patient with others, we develop strong and loyal relationships with our peers. We also will be recipients of the patience of others when we need it, for we will reap what we sow.

Be Prayerful
It is difficult for a person who has been in regular, daily communion with Jesus Christ to be short, unkind, or uncaring toward others. It is not impossible, but it is difficult. We all sometimes stumble and fail to live up to our ideals. But we immediately sense conviction for our conduct when we have fallen short of presenting a Christlike spirit. Spending time in the presence of the Lord humbles us and keeps us mindful of the fragile human state and the significant needs of others.

> This world will have its full share of difficulties (John 16:33), but the believer is to be steadfast in time of trouble. The realization that life is to some

extent an obstacle course keeps a person from being surprised when things do not go as planned. Afflictions are to be borne patiently. And the source of spiritual help during such times is prayer. So Paul counseled his readers, "Steadfastly maintain the habit of prayer" (Phillips). Barclay comments, "No man should be surprised when life collapses if he insists on living it alone" (Barclay, Romans, 166). Most Christians will confess the difficulty of maintaining a regular and effective prayer life. The reason is not difficult to discern. If Satan can keep us out of touch with God, he will not have to worry about any trouble we might cause for his evil kingdom. (Robert H. Mounce, Romans, vol. 27, The New American Commentary [Nashville: Broadman & Holman Publishers, 1995], 238)

Being prayerful aligns our hearts and spirits with that of the Lord, and it enables us to appreciate and practice the highest measures of ethical behavior. A prayerful person naturally cares about others and wants to give no one cause to reproach the name of Jesus Christ. Consequently, his conduct is genuine and honest with love and care toward everyone.

Be Hospitable

Graciousness and hospitality are warming and welcoming traits, which Paul encouraged in Romans 12:13: "given to hospitality." However, one might wonder, *Does that mean I am supposed to take strangers into my home*? Not necessarily. The word is translated from the Greek word *philoxenos*, which means "hospitality, care to strangers" (James Swanson,

Dictionary of Biblical Languages with Semantic Domains: Greek [New Testament] [Oak Harbor: Logos Research Systems, Inc., 1997]).

In the days Paul wrote to the Romans, providing lodging to strangers traveling through was common, and it was an aspect of hospitality. However, the idea of the word is to exercise "care to strangers." Today it would not always translate into providing overnight lodging for others. More often, it would have to do with our treatment of strangers—truly and genuinely caring about and for their needs. Hospitality could take on the form of a special offering or a warm meal or sharing a little time of fellowship. It involves seeing their need and caring enough to reach out to them in an effort to minister to their need.

One thing is certain. If we care enough about people to minister to their needs with warmth and kindness, our hospitality will impact them positively. The door of relationship will swing wide open and we will have the opportunity to minister to their hurting and suffering heart.

Bless Others
We should make an effort to be a blessing to others and not a curse. (See Romans 12:14.) Through the godly characteristics with which God endows believers, they are able to bless people and demonstrate good and ethical Christian kindness. In a day of a "get even" mentality, we reflect Christ to this world when we refrain from exercising vengeance against others. Even when others have mistreated or abused us, it pays to bless them with kindness. (See Romans 12:19.) It is not easy to pray blessing upon those who are unkind to us, but such is the heart of true Christianity.

Bless them that curse you, and pray for them which
despitefully use you. (Luke 6:28)

(See also Matthew 5:44.)

Be Compassionate and Sensitive

Paul wrote, "Rejoice with them that do rejoice, and weep with
them that weep" (Romans 12:15). We should be compassionate
and sensitive toward what others are feeling and experiencing,
whether it involves great joy or terrible sorrow. Whatever they
are experiencing, we should positively impact them through
spiritual compassion.

Pastors often find themselves dealing with this very thing.
They might leave one hospital room where a family is weeping
to go to another room where a family is rejoicing. One family
has lost a loved one to death, but a young couple is jubilant
over the arrival of a baby. The pastor weeps with those who
are suffering, but with others he or she is laughing, smiling,
and posing for pictures. The pastor has to be sensitive to the
needs of people and the situation at hand. The people involved
in each case have authentic feelings and genuine needs. Ethics
involves understanding the appropriate conduct for each
individual circumstance.

Many of these characteristics Paul wrote about in Romans
12 may not translate directly into ethical conduct. Still, they
all have a role in forming and shaping relationships. Following
these principles will lead a person to treat individuals ethically,
which will foster growing and reciprocal, healthy relationships.

Be Fair and Equitable

Romans 12:16 mentions three vital attitudes to dealing ethically with our peers. The first principle comes from the first sentence: "Be of the same mind one toward another." This sentence speaks of treating people with fairness and equity.

It is such a turnoff when someone treats us one way and then turns to another person and treats that one differently—possibly even ignoring us. What an uncomfortable feeling! We ought to treat all people with kindness and fairness, making no difference between personalities. Every individual deserves basic, fundamental respect, and when we respect that person we gain his or her mutual respect and build rapport.

Have you ever been in a crowd talking with someone, but you noticed the person seemed distracted while talking to you? It seemed as if he or she was looking for someone else, giving you the sense the individual was not engaged in the conversation with you. Possibly, it caused you to feel denigrated and devalued. In all relationships, we should be fair and equitable with every person, for all individuals have value and deserve at least a minimum measure of respect.

Condescend to Others, but without Condescension

The second idea the apostle brought out in Romans 12:16 comes from the second sentence: "Mind not high things, but condescend to men of low estate." It sounds like a paradox, yet we should "condescend" to all people regardless of their status in life and never with an attitude of "condescension." Whether the person is one of high estate ("mind not high things") or low estate, the person is worthy of proper treatment. He or she will immediately recognize when a person possesses a condescending attitude.

The English Standard Version of Scripture translates the verse as follows: "Live in harmony with one another. Do not be haughty, but associate with the lowly. Never be wise in your own sight" (Romans 12:16). Haughtiness puts off people and disgusts them. We are to associate with all people, whatever their state in life may be. And we should always emanate a spirit of humility, never arrogance.

Perhaps the definitions for *condescend* from *Merriam-Webster Dictionary* would add some clarity here: "to descend to a less formal or dignified level. . . . to waive the privileges of rank. . . . to assume an air of superiority." So there are a couple different ideas included in the word condescension.

We should waive perceived privileges of rank that we may effectively associate with all people and never exhibit an air of superiority. A humble attitude and approach toward people will win many loyal friends, but arrogance will turn people away. Incidentally, Paul made an inference to arrogance and conceit in the third sentence of verse 16.

Avoid Arrogance and Self-Conceitedness

Paul wrote, "Be not wise in your own conceits." Nobody enjoys being around a know-it-all braggart. Some people's opinion of themselves is so high they devalue the knowledge of others and think no one else can do anything right. Or at least they think no one can do it as well as they can do it. They denigrate the opinion of others and are so arrogant they are insulting.

If a Christian truly desires to make a difference in his or her world, one should avoid arrogance and self-conceit. We do not have to put ourselves down, but neither should we think more highly of ourselves than we ought to think (Romans 12:3).

Be Honest Always

Finally, Paul underscored once again one of the primary essentials of ethical conduct: honesty. We should always be honest in every dealing we have with others. "Recompense to no man evil for evil. Provide things honest in the sight of all men" (Romans 12:17).

There is never an excuse for dishonesty among Christians. A Christian should always be completely forthright and honest in all his or her dealings. We should not even frame our words deceptively so as to lead a person to reach a false conclusion. Complete honesty is a foundation stone of Christian ethics.

Overpower Evil with Good

Paul summed up his discourse on proper ethical conduct and characteristics that facilitate good relationships with one's peers. Paul urged the Romans: "Be not overcome of evil, but overcome evil with good" (Romans 12:21). One key to having good relationships with one's peers is in overpowering evil with good characteristics. The characteristics and principles mentioned in Romans 12, which are empowered through the Holy Spirit, will help us to do that.

If we will treat all people the same with genuineness, honesty, kindness, sensitivity, and patience, avoiding arrogance or conceit, we will never lack for friends. Our relationships can be exactly as the Lord designed and desired them to be, with candid and ethical conduct in all things.

CHAPTER SIX

ETHICS IN VERTICAL RELATIONSHIPS— LEADERS IN AUTHORITY

Dietrich Bonhoeffer, in his book *Ethics*, makes an interesting observation: "The tree of knowledge of Good and Evil produced the ability to choose our own good or our own evil. Both choices may take us equally distant from God. We have a third alternative, God's will."

Some individuals may think ethics is all about submission to authority, but it is not. Ethics is about proper conduct toward everyone, whoever that person may be. He or she might occupy a position of authority over us, be a peer, or be one under our authority in either spiritual or secular life. It is important that a person "of authority" understands how to conduct himself toward others—including those who are under his authority.

It is important for one "under authority" to conduct himself properly toward his authority figures. Vertical relationships move in both directions, up and down.

TOUCH NOT GOD'S ANOINTED

The story of David and Saul well illustrates one of the most prominent principles regarding respectful ethics in the way we deal with spiritual authorities. This is especially true of the story that relates their encounter at a cave in Engedi. (See I Samuel 24:1–22 and the brief discussion in chapter 2 of this book.) The story communicates an ethical principle of Scripture, the violation of which invites tragedy. To follow the principle of due respect is an essential element of success in Christian living, and in life in general to a great degree.

We are to restrain ourselves from being disrespectful toward those in spiritual authority over us. The principle also extends to authority figures in the natural or physical realm. For instance, consider Paul's exchange as recorded in Acts 23:

> And looking intently at the council, Paul said, "Brothers, I have lived my life before God in all good conscience up to this day." And the high priest Ananias commanded those who stood by him to strike him on the mouth. Then Paul said to him, "God is going to strike you, you whitewashed wall! Are you sitting to judge me according to the law, and yet contrary to the law you order me to be struck?" Those who stood by said, "Would you revile God's high priest?" And Paul said, "I did not know, brothers, that he was the high priest, for it is

written, 'You shall not speak evil of a ruler of your people.'" (Acts 23:1–5, ESV)

(See Exodus 22:28; Ecclesiastes 10:20.)

In addressing the matter of showing due respect in our ethical approach to others, Peter stated, "But chiefly them that walk after the flesh in the lust of uncleanness, and despise government. Presumptuous are they, selfwilled, they are not afraid to speak evil of dignities" (II Peter 2:10). We are not to speak evil of the reputation of others, which includes those who are in authority over us, whether spiritual or secular. Interestingly, the KJV word "dignities" in verse 10 is translated from the same Greek word, *doxa*, which also is translated as "glory." *The Theological Lexicon of the New Testament* defines the word as "expectation, opinion, reputation, honor, glory" (Ceslas Spicq and James D. Ernest, *Theological Lexicon of the New Testament* [Peabody, MA: Hendrickson Publishers, 1994], 362).

According to Paul, it is inexcusable for believers to attack the reputation of others, which is translated in the KJV as "speak evil." When we have differences with those who are in authority over us, there is a correct way to go about resolving those differences. The correct way never includes speaking to or about them with disrespect.

God sets up and takes down leaders and rulers in this world—both spiritual and secular. We may elect certain leaders, but God puts it in the people's hearts to elevate specific individuals for particular seasons of time. It is He who directs the affairs of humankind. (See Job 12:18; Psalm 75:7; Daniel

2:21; 4:17.) "The lot is cast into the lap, but its every decision is from the LORD" (Proverbs 16:33, ESV).

It is overwhelmingly presumptuous for a fallible human being to believe he knows better than the Lord! If God has elevated a person to leadership, who are we to denigrate and disrespect the person? Even when such an individual is wrong as was the case with Saul, we must respect and submit to that person to whatever degree is possible. We must wait for God to take care of the matter in His timing. For however long that season of leadership may rest upon that individual, he or she is ordained by God for that role. We are not to lay one hand upon the person. Further, telling inappropriate jokes about a widely disrespected leader falls beneath the measure of respect God has ordained. Even if we cannot respect the person because of his or her conduct, we must respect the position and authority one holds.

RELATIONSHIP TO AUTHORITY

God ordained and instituted authority—both spiritual and secular—in order to facilitate a life of peace, harmony, and lawfulness. To examine a biblical perspective of authority, one could look to Paul's writing in Romans 13:1–8. There he addressed the responsibility all individuals have to submit to authorities: "Let every person be subject to the governing authorities. For there is no authority except from God, and those that exist have been instituted by God. Therefore whoever resists the authorities resists what God has appointed, and those who resist will incur judgment" (Romans 13:1–2, ESV).

Paul goes on to explain that figures of authority are not a terror to those who do right, but to those who work evil. Paul even called secular individuals who execute authority "ministers of God." They are performing a service that was planned and ordained by the Almighty in order to structure life and provide for general peace and harmony. This is even true of officials who collect taxes from taxpaying citizens.

> Render therefore to all their dues: tribute to whom tribute is due; custom to whom custom; fear to whom fear; honour to whom honour. (Romans 13:7)

Throughout the entire social structure on earth, God has established authority for our good. These vertical relationships involve ones who are under our authority and those to whom we answer in subjection. The appropriate attitude toward those over us or under us is that of respect.

RESPECT FOR AND CONDUCT TOWARD AUTHORITY

In Titus 3, Paul described the conduct Christians should exhibit, which also would govern their conduct toward those in authority. (See Titus 3:1–7.) Christians are to be subject to "principalities and powers," that is, to "rulers and authorities" (ESV, NKJV). Some of the characteristics of Christian respect and conduct toward authority are as follows.

- Submissive
- Obedient
- Not Critical
- Peaceful
- Gentle
- Meek and Humble

We are to be submissive to authority and avoid rebellion. Let us look more closely at these two opposing attitudes and their relationship to authority.

Submission to Authority and Ordinances

Submission is a concept that many in this postmodern culture do not like. People are strongly opinionated and individualistic. Many reject the idea of being told what they need to do, much less being told what they will do.

There are at least four things individuals need to understand about submission to authority:

> 1. *Being submissive does not equal being a "pushover."* A person does not have to abandon his or her individuality. The world has made submission to appear as weakness. But a strong, individualistic person can still be submissive to his or her authorities, and biblically, he or she is required to possess such an attitude.

> 2. *Being submissive is beneficial to the one submitting.* There are definite, promised benefits to living the Christian life with submission to authority. Submission brings blessing to the ones who humble themselves with contrite compliance.

> 3. *Being submissive involves a person's spirit and attitude as much, if not more than his or her actions.*

> 4. *Being submissive is the Lord's plan and it pleases Him.* (See I Peter 2:13–18; Titus 3; Romans 13.)

Submission pleases God because it both reflects and disciplines a person's spirit and attitude, which are vitally involved in a person's salvation. They do not *effect* salvation, because salvation is by grace through faith in Jesus Christ as a person experiences the plan of salvation. However, a person's spirit and attitude definitely do *affect* his or her salvation. A bitter and rancorous spirit will distract a person from the beauty of salvation and get that individual focused on harmful things. It can cause him or her to stumble and fail to continue serving Jesus Christ. If a person's spirit and attitude are sweet, humble, and properly submitted to others, that individual will be more inclined to pursue holy and godly interests. Individuals with the right attitude will be less distracted and drawn away from that which strengthens their relationship with Christ.

To fail to exhibit a submissive spirit will turn an individual toward rebellion. To reject one mandate of Scripture is rebellious and it opens the door to more rebellion and the rejection of all scriptural teachings.

Rebellion

In II Peter 2:9–22, Peter continued his writings concerning speaking evil of ones in leadership. Notice the wisdom exercised by angels toward leaders and the strong destruction suffered by those individuals who lack such foresight:

> Then the Lord knows how to deliver the godly out of temptations and to reserve the unjust under punishment for the day of judgment, and especially those who walk according to the flesh in the lust of uncleanness and despise authority. They are presumptuous, self-willed. They are not afraid

to speak evil of dignitaries, whereas angels, who are greater in power and might, do not bring a reviling accusation against them before the Lord. But these, like natural brute beasts made to be caught and destroyed, speak evil of the things they do not understand, and will utterly perish in their own corruption, and will receive the wages of unrighteousness, as those who count it pleasure to carouse in the daytime. (II Peter 2:9–13, ESV)

Jude also wrote and warned of those who "despise dominion, and speak evil of dignities" (Jude 8). (See also Jude 9–22.) Rebellion is a serious and dangerous departure from the ways of the Lord. Further, the Lord has associated rebellion with witchcraft. "For rebellion is as the sin of witchcraft, and stubbornness is as iniquity and idolatry. Because thou hast rejected the word of the LORD, He hath also rejected thee from being king" (I Samuel 15:23).

When reading the story of David and King Saul, we read about an amazing conclusion to the entire saga. David recognized the danger of rebellion against Saul even though Saul was in the wrong and David was in the right. David felt convicted for even cutting off a portion of Saul's garment to demonstrate his character and discipline in not harming the king. While David avoided the pitfall of rebellion, however, Saul fell headlong into it. God cursed him and rejected him from his position of authority. In both cases we see clearly demonstrated the seriousness of rebellion. One provides a positive example in avoiding rebellion and the other a negative example of the seriousness of it. It is as wrong and deadly as the sin of witchcraft!

David's deliverance from Saul and promotion to leadership within the kingdom did not come overnight, but God eventually elevated David to the throne. David did right by keeping his spirit and attitude toward Saul in check, despite Saul tormenting him and hunting him like an animal.

No matter the perceptions of right and wrong, we are to avoid rebellion at all costs. As long as a person occupies a position of authority in our lives, we are to show deference and due respect. We must resist all urges to rebel against the individual's authority. However, leaders should take note of Saul's life. The anointing of leadership is no excuse for rebellion against God in exercising one's authority. It matters how the leader practices authority as well as how the follower submits to it.

NOT AS LORDS OVER GOD'S HERITAGE

Peter clearly expressed the responsibilities of leaders who have oversight of the "flock of God," that is, the individuals in his or her congregation. We know these individuals as pastors, assistant pastors, and similarly positioned leaders in the local church.

> The elders which are among you I exhort. . . . Feed the flock of God which is among you, taking the oversight thereof, not by constraint, but willingly; not for filthy lucre, but of a ready mind; neither as being lords over God's heritage, but being ensamples to the flock. (I Peter 5:1–3)

The Lord gives authority to spiritual leaders to help facilitate order and unity within the corporate functions of the church, the body of Christ. While it is imperative those under their authority respond properly to that authority, it also is vital these spiritual leaders exercise their authority properly. What is the appropriate approach to exercising the Lord's authority? Basically, it involves possessing and exhibiting the same spirit and attitude expected from those under their authority, such as respect, honor, integrity, and humility.

Peter indicated leaders are not set up as lords over the heritage of God. They have much the same responsibilities toward their subordinates as the subordinates have toward them. Christian leaders must never forget whose church this is: it is the Lord's church, not theirs. The Lord purchased the church with His own precious blood. He has given His leaders specific roles and responsibilities, but how they conduct themselves in leading others is a serious matter.

I knew a leader once who wanted a particular wall inside the facilities relocated. While discussing the relocation with several men under his authority, the men pointed out reasons they thought it was not a good idea. During the course of the discussion, the leader simply walked over to the wall and put his foot through it. As the drywall dust was still settling, he looked at the men and said, "Move the wall!" The discussion was over.

The leader had the authority with these men to make the decision, but his display of arrogance and authority was anything but Christlike. He rudely exhibited anger, arrogance, and stubbornness. He showed no compassion, humility, or understanding in his exercise of leadership. In his exercise of authority he was guilty of abuse. The men under his authority were accountable to God to be submissive, but the one in authority was also accountable to use his authority correctly.

Perhaps he was frustrated. Possibly he was tired and at a loss as to how to lead his subordinates, but his actions crossed the line.

Abuse of authority carries its own penalties. Secular leaders will suffer natural or organizational reprisals for poor leadership, possibly including demotion. Spiritual leaders will possibly give an account to congregational or organizational leaders who are over them when they abuse their power. All will give an account to God as to how they used authority. We all shall give an account to God for our attitudes and actions. (See Romans 10:10–13.)

RESPECT IS A TWO-WAY STREET

Religious figure Gordon B. Hinckley stated, "Where ever the spirit of Christ is known, there is much of good will, of mutual respect, of love and appreciation and kindness" (http://www. brainyquote.com, accessed June 14, 2016). Certainly, that is how relationships within the body of Christ should be. Unfortunately, we are human and sometimes say things or express attitudes that fail to reflect Christ's love and kindness. Still, if we want to be respected by others who are under our authority, we must be careful to exhibit respect in our dealings with them. Respect must be mutual to work effectively.

When a leader demands respect and honor, he is most likely not to receive it. Or if he receives the demanded honor and respect, it probably is superficial because people do not respect those who demand it. They respect those who earn it. How do we earn respect from others? We earn respect by giving it away—and also by being respectable.

Ethics in vertical relationships of authority extend both upward and downward. Proper ethical conduct is required by all who are in a relationship regardless of authority status. We must respect, honor, and give deference to leaders, but they also must treat with respect those under their oversight. They must exercise diligent and ethical behavior that exhibits only the highest levels of consideration. Otherwise, they will plant seeds of resentment in their charges and the relationship will break down and eventually fall apart.

CHAPTER SEVEN

ETHICAL CONDUCT TOWARD THOSE OF THE OPPOSITE SEX

> Now concerning the things whereof ye wrote unto me: It is good for a man not to touch a woman. Nevertheless, to avoid fornication, let every man have his own wife, and let every woman have her own husband. (I Corinthians 7:1)

In his first epistle to the believers in Corinth, Paul apparently began to answer some questions they had posed to him regarding marriage and sexual relations. Paul opened chapter 7 with a startling statement: "It is good for a man not to touch a woman." What did Paul mean and what applications might his words have for us today?

Without entering into a lengthy theological discussion, most commentators observe that Paul was talking about the benefits of being single. However, in the subsequent verses he made it clear he was in no way denigrating marriage or sexual relations within marriage. Nevertheless, the many dynamics of marriage, including sexual relations, require individuals to follow vital, specific biblical guidelines for marriage and sex.

What is intriguing, however, is that the root of the Greek word Paul utilized came to be used on occasion as an "idiom to refer to having sexual intercourse with a woman" (John D. Barry, Douglas Mangum, Derek R. Brown, et al., *Faithlife Study Bible* [Bellingham, WA: Lexham Press, 2012, 2016], I Corinthians 7:1). Another commentator referred to it as a "euphemism for sexual intercourse" (David K. Lowery, "1 Corinthians," in *The Bible Knowledge Commentary: An Exposition of the Scriptures*, eds. J. F. Walvoord and R. B. Zuck, vol. 2 [Wheaton, IL: Victor Books, 1985], 517).

When Paul said it is good for a man not "to touch" a woman, he used the Greek word *hapto*. Of the forty times a form of this word is used in the Greek New Testament, thirty-four times the basic meaning of the word is simply "to handle (touch)." Four times the word is used with the idea "to kindle," such as kindling a fire. One time the word is used in the sense of "affecting negatively, lay hold of," and the remaining time it meant "to have intercourse, handle a woman" (Definitions from Faithlife Corporation. "Logos Bible Software Bible Sense Lexicon." Logos Bible Software, Computer software. Bellingham, WA: Faithlife Corporation, September 17, 2016).

It does not take a highly skilled or educated philosopher or psychologist to recognize how the idea of "to touch" became an idiom or euphemism for sexual contact, the context in which Paul used the word. The point in bringing up this passage and its correlating discussion is simply this: the problem or danger to which Paul alluded in I Corinthians 7:1 does not begin with the act of sexual intercourse; it begins with an act of inappropriately touching a person of the opposite sex.

Humans are wired with certain built-in reactors that automatically respond to the stimuli of touching another human. Those reactors are different based on many contributing factors, but because of the natural and normal role God gave humans in procreating and populating the earth (Genesis 1:28), many acts of touch between a man and a woman can activate the sexual senses, leading to temptation at best and immorality at worst whenever that touch is inappropriate—that which is between two unmarried individuals.

When my girls were teenagers, my wife and I strongly counseled them against the casual touching we were observing between teenagers of opposite sexes. The touching we saw was not meant to be inappropriate, per se; the teens seemed to be innocent in the way they touched each other. However, because of the way the human body responds to touch, they were opening doors of unnecessary and unwise temptation.

On one occasion of discussing the matter with my daughters, their response was something along the line of, "Dad, you don't trust us." I responded, "I do trust you. But I do not trust the flesh and I do not trust the devil." In other words, our flesh will react in certain, pre-wired, preprogrammed responses to human touch, and Satan will exploit those natural responses and take advantage of the affected normal and innocent feelings and emotions.

Since believers understand they have these human, fleshly tendencies, it is imperative that they expend the extra effort and exercise the additional precautions necessary to safeguard their emotions and protect themselves from temptation and deception. In this chapter, we will endeavor to consider some practical precautions for managing our conduct around and with those of the opposite sex.

First, let us consider some principles that apply to both sexes and to all individuals regardless of whether they are single, married, layperson, or minister.

GENERAL CONSIDERATIONS FOR BOTH SEXES

Honor and Respect. The first principle to which we should give careful attention, both men and women, is that of treating all people with due honor and respect. We all are made in the image of God and deserve to be viewed and treated with the utmost measure of honor and respect.

One of the most serious problems with the prevalence of pornography in our culture today is that it objectifies individuals, whether it is female-oriented pornography or male-oriented pornography. It treats invaluable humans made in the image of God as though they were mere objects created for the selfish pleasure of another person. Pornography disrespects the beautiful and holy creation of the Almighty, and consequently dishonors and disrespects God Himself.

Respect causes an individual to view and treat all people honorably. It would never allow us to take advantage of others by attempting to satisfy our selfish and ambitious human desires at the expense of another. That is exactly what a person does to one of the opposite sex when he or she attempts to gain personal gratification without regard for the other individual as a divine creation of God.

Consider a rare and very valuable piece of art. Realizing its value, we would never treat it carelessly. We would make certain it is protected from the elements by keeping it in storage that includes a climate-controlled environment. We would guard it by keeping it out of the reach of children who would not understand its value, and we would safeguard it against theft or vandalism. What causes us to treat it with such care? We have great respect for it because of our knowledge of its great value.

So it should be with how we view and treat members of the opposite sex. We recognize their value as being divinely created by the same God who created us. We view them with worth and exceptional value in the eyes of God. We know they do not exist for our pleasure, but for God's. (See Colossians 1:16.) Such respect compels us to treat them accordingly with honor and respect.

One way a man shows his respect for women is by avoiding the temptation to eye and ogle at every immodest girl who walks by. First of all, his conduct is disrespectful toward God and toward himself. He is allowing himself to fall prey to temptation through his visual senses. However, his lustful conduct is also disrespectful toward women in general and certainly toward any woman in whose company he may be at the time. This kind of conduct causes modest girls to feel devalued and unappreciated because of their modesty. Instead of disrespecting modest ladies, he should be supporting their godly efforts and treating them as the human treasures they are indeed. Whatever measures he must take, he should fight the battle of his eyes and mind, keeping them focused on that which is pure, wholesome, and godly—and refusing to allow his eyes to dwell upon the ungodly sight of immodest and provocatively dressed women.

Because of the way they are divinely wired, women tend to have much less of a problem with the temptation to lustfully gawk at good-looking men. Still, the principles remain the same. Women are to respect men by avoiding the lustful observation of ones whom they might consider to be "hunks." And as is the case with men, they should support and cherish men who make sincere efforts to dress and behave themselves in a modest and godly fashion.

Conscious of Propriety in Conduct and Appearance. Whether a person is single or married, there are situations he or she should avoid for the sake of what is appropriate or inappropriate. In addition to avoiding impropriety, individuals should avoid circumstances that even have an appearance of questionable ethics. The Scriptures teach us to "abstain from all appearance of evil" (I Thessalonians 5:22). One might question, "What is inappropriate and what situations could appear to lack propriety?" Consider the following few examples.

Couples Together Alone in Non-Public Places. Whether or not they are dating, a man and a woman being together in a private space opens the door to temptation. Sometimes meetings or work situations may create circumstances in which a couple is suddenly alone. To protect both their emotions as well as their reputations, they should seek out a public setting for the completion of their work or meeting if at all possible. It is not worth risking your human resolve in temptation, and it is not worth destroying your good reputation. Further, none of us are immune to temptation and all are capable of falling into immorality.

Touching Each Other, Even in Non-Sexual and Affirming Ways. As mentioned earlier, the human touch is potent stimuli that triggers powerful, involuntary emotional and physical responses in the human body. Touching and hugging is very common in today's business world, but it is dangerous between men and women who are unmarried or not married to each other.

I recently was at the airport waiting for my wife to exit the secure area of the concourse. While waiting, I observed three obvious coworkers who had apparently arrived home from a business trip together. Before going their separate ways, each one hugged the others. Admittedly, their conduct was probably innocent and free from sexual overtones. They appeared to be members of a company team who had spent the day conducting business together out of town. Their hugs were undoubtedly intended to convey camaraderie, friendship, and unity of goals between the individual team members. However, if one or more of the three were having marital problems at home, just an innocent hug from a coworker could throw open a door to temptation. It could even lead the troubled party to seek intimacy outside of his or her marriage and could lead the involved individuals into infidelity.

Out-of-town Business Trips. In today's business world, it is not uncommon to have to go out of town on business with associates. Sometimes that could involve a man-and-woman team, either unmarried or married to others. It might be impossible to avoid such a situation in one's particular line of work; however, a believer can take steps to safeguard himself or herself and avoid an unpleasant or compromising situation.

First, the public plane ride should not be problematic as long as the coworkers conduct themselves professionally with public decorum. Both are in a public setting conducting work in public, including their means of public transportation. Still, they should make certain they guard their conduct so as not to send any unintentional signals through flirtatious behavior or give the impression they might be open to advances by their business partner.

Second, it is important to avoid eating meals together as a couple. Sometimes that is difficult and it probably means the believer will have to eat alone. However, a meal shared by two individuals—even though they are in a public restaurant—can too quickly become intimate in conversation and can expose one or both individuals to a very uncomfortable situation or possible temptation. One should eat alone or in larger groups. If necessary, one could order room service and eat alone in his or her hotel room. We should avoid temptation at all costs and avoid even what could appear questionable to others.

Third, we should keep all business meetings and work in public places, avoiding all situations that would cause the two business partners to be alone in a private space.

Fourth, if possible, perhaps the believer's spouse could accompany the team on the business trip. It could be expensive since it would have to be at one's personal expense, and it might not even be possible due to the spouse's responsibilities at home. Still, if it were possible, it could certainly defuse many potential problems of conducting business away from home.

Finally, we should guard our words. We should avoid all language that could appear flirtatious or playful. Even innocent words spoken too casually or playfully can convey the wrong idea to one's business partner and can invite unwanted advances.

In addition to these general considerations, let us observe some specific advice for those who are single and are around members of the opposite sex.

ADDITIONAL CONSIDERATIONS FOR THE UNMARRIED

Courtship. Dating can be a beautiful experience in which two individuals explore common interests and learn about the personality, likes, and dislikes of each other. Some have stated that individuals should never date a person whom they would not marry. That does not mean two dating individuals will marry, but it means they are in the process of seriously exploring the possibilities of a long-term relationship. When thinking of dating in this way, one could ask himself or herself, "How would I want someone to treat the person who will one day become my husband or my wife?"

Conduct. Both guys and girls should treat their dates with the utmost honor and respect. They should be courteous and thoughtful. They should have a good time and enjoy one another's company, but they should go out of their way to avoid intimate speech, questionable conduct, being in private spaces alone, or touching their date in any way—even seemingly innocent and nonsexual ways. One should not try to see how sexy or flirtatious he or she can be without crossing a line of impropriety. One should always keep a distance from the cultural and spiritual lines of what could be perceived as unacceptable or questionable conduct. A believer should always act with class, honor, and respect.

Dress. It should go without saying, but both guys and girls should never push the limits of decency, modesty, or propriety in their dress. One should not dress in any way that could be perceived as flirtatious, immodest, or provocative. If one dresses or acts trashy, that one should not be surprised when he or she is treated in a trashy way by others. The way we dress reveals our respect for God, for ourselves, and also for the one whom we are courting.

Self-Imposed Curfew. It is beyond the scope of this writing to try to establish an acceptable curfew for all dating couples. Many factors could and should enter into the idea of setting a curfew. However, it is advisable for single, dating individuals to establish self-imposed curfews. For them it is not a matter of *having* to be in by a certain time, but a matter of *needing* a predetermined time at which they will conclude a pleasant evening with their date. Having this predetermined time established sets personal boundaries before the date even begins. The individual knows—and possibly relays to his or her date if needful—that he or she needs to be home by a certain hour. It places self-imposed limits on time, which aids a person in self-governing himself or herself while out on a date. The best kind of discipline is self-discipline and those who observe our behavior, including dating partners, will respect us and appreciate us more for exercising that kind of self-control.

In addition to these practical considerations for the unmarried, consider some additional suggestions for those who are married.

ADDITIONAL CONSIDERATIONS FOR THE MARRIED

Married men and women also have responsibilities toward the opposite sex in their dress, speech, mannerisms, and conduct.

Married couples must establish and maintain clear boundaries in their marriage. For example, they should conduct themselves with discretion and propriety when in the company of other couples whether those couples are married or single. Because of the intimate relationship a married couple enjoys with each other, they may be tempted to become lax in the discipline of their conduct in the presence of others.

Couples Must Discipline Their Speech Around Others. It is one thing to share playful comments when alone as a married couple, but it becomes altogether different when the couple is in the presence of others. They should never allow their speech to have even a taint of discolor, suggestiveness, or inappropriate language in such settings.

Their speech and actions should always be respectful toward others, considering the needs and feelings of others. They should never cross lines of inappropriate conduct when they are in the presence of others—especially when in the presence of those of the opposite sex. They should always be cautious that they say and do the right things and avoid all questionable conduct.

Couples should guard their conversations among other couples. One problem for couples is that they too often let down their guard when two or more couples are together for fellowship. In the playfulness and lightheartedness of the occasion, a person might think it is all right in the presence of his or her spouse to cross lines he or she would never ordinarily cross. Crossing such lines of propriety is still wrong—even with other couples and in the presence of one's own spouse. We should never even open a door to temptation by discussing things that are inappropriate for public discussion between members of opposite sexes. Couples should never become too familiar in their conversations with other couples.

Couples Should Strictly Avoid Being Alone with Others of the Opposite Sex Except for Their Companion. Neither partner should ever allow himself or herself to be drawn into a compromising situation for any reason. Sometimes it may seem to make sense to spend time alone with another of the opposite sex in order to accomplish assigned work or shared duties, but it is unwise and inappropriate. Being alone with one of the opposite sex who is not one's spouse opens a person up to a soiled reputation at best and to temptation and moral failure at worst. Because we are human, all temptation has the potential to distract us from spirituality, to draw us into sinful conduct, and to destroy us through unfaithfulness to our companion. Even honorable work and worthy causes cannot justify being alone with a person of the opposite sex other than one's own husband or wife.

Couples Should Strongly Discipline Themselves Regarding Their Entertainment. That a couple is married does not make right the watching of pornographic or questionable movies. With the prevalence of entertainment through video and online streaming, a couple may be tempted to partake of media they would not otherwise consume. They might reason to themselves, "It's only the two of us in the intimacy of our home. It could be stimulating to our intimacy as a couple." What that couple might not realize is that they still are subjecting themselves to inappropriate temptations. Further, if the source of entertainment has vulgar language or suggestive scenes, they are planting those words and pictures in their mind that will remain with them indefinitely. That the couple is married and alone does not change the fundamentals of what is right and wrong, appropriate and inappropriate. They owe it to themselves personally and to their companion the godly respect of refusing to partake of any questionable so-called entertainment.

Couples Should Carefully Monitor the Use of Computers and Internet in Their Home. Online pornography and chat rooms have destroyed far too many marriages, including marriages between Christians. It is too easy for well-meaning believers to expose themselves to temptation and end up falling into sinful behaviors that can unalterably destroy them as individuals, as well as devastate their marriage and families. They should utilize some of the practical Internet safeguards that are frequently mentioned today. They should take seriously their responsibility to protect themselves and their homes. For example, they may consider the use of Internet filters on their computers as well as locating computer stations in open and public areas of the home. It is also wise to place restrictive hours on the use of the computers.

ADDITIONAL CONSIDERATIONS FOR MINISTERS

Because of the nature of Christian ministry, all of these principles guiding one's ethical conduct become exponentially vital to ministers. It is impossible to overemphasize the importance of ministers guarding their conduct toward those of the opposite sex. One small crack of careless conduct or ethical breach can quickly become a chasm of destruction to the minister as a person, to his or her ministry, and to those who are within that minister's spectrum of influence.

Ministers must exemplify the highest standards of the morality and virtues they proclaim to others from God's Word. They challenge others to follow biblical principles, but do they themselves follow those same principles?

Paul mentioned a number of virtues required in those who give oversight in ministry. Specifically, he connected the virtues to those seeking the office of a bishop; however,

INTEGRITY

his reference to that particular office is broader than it may immediately appear. The word "bishop" is translated from the Greek *episkopos*, which generally means "overseer" or "watcher" (Kittel, Gerhard, Geoffrey W. Bromiley, and Gerhard Friedrich, eds. *Theological Dictionary of the New Testament.* Grand Rapids, MI: Eerdmans, 1964–). Books have been written on how I Timothy 3 may be interpreted and applied. Certainly, Paul's words apply primarily to pastors as they oversee the spiritual welfare of others. However, it seems completely reasonable and a permissible use of episkopos to apply the virtues Paul mentioned in a general sense to all ministers. All ministers bear influence upon the people of God, and in their specific areas of influence they are accountable to God for their conduct and leadership.

In addition to qualities that pertain to one's calling and abilities, the qualifications Paul mentioned in I Timothy 3:1–7 govern a person's personal conduct and reputation. Clearly, those who seek to lead others through Christian ministry carry significant responsibility to God and will be accountable ultimately to Him. It is important that ministers maintain a high standard so they may positively and effectively lead and influence other believers in their relationship with Jesus Christ.

SINGLE MINISTERS
Whether they are male or female, single ministers must exercise great care to maintain a godly reputation. Let us consider some of the high ethical standards ministers should maintain as they pertain to those of the opposite sex.

Friendships. Whatever their ministerial involvement may be, because they are single they will naturally be interested in developing relationships with those of the opposite sex. Often, those relationships are strictly platonic and they develop through mutual friends or common interests. These kinds of relationships are healthy and beneficial to the overall personal growth and development of a minister of either sex; however, they also raise the need for caution between the friends to safeguard their hearts and reputations.

Because these friends are of opposite sexes, they must follow the guidelines outlined in the sections above for the sake of their individual reputations and ministerial effectiveness. They cannot afford to be alone in private spaces out of the public eye. They may have absolutely no romantically inclined interest in each other; they may just be friends. Still, temptations can arise even out of innocent encounters and their relationship with Christ and reputation among people are too valuable to risk ruin. It is wise and safe to follow the highest possible standards of conduct.

It is also vital to recognize that platonic relationships sometimes develop into romantic interests. This is neither unusual nor unhealthy. They often become best friends, giving spiritual intimacy the opportunity to develop. Then it is possible that one day they discover their interest in each other has become something that is more than platonic and spiritual friendship; they may discover in each other the kind of person they would like to spend a lifetime with, and their friendship turns toward romantic friendship. Such a transition ratchets up the need to safeguard their conduct lest they fall into temptation in a moment of unanticipated weakness.

Dating. It is normal for single ministers to desire to date ones of the opposite sex. They are human, and the call of God upon their lives does not eliminate their natural human desires for friendship and intimacy in a lifetime companion. Dating is the pathway to discovering and developing that kind of a relationship. However, ministers carry a greater burden of responsibility when it comes to dating and conducting relationships with those of the opposite sex. They must be exceptionally cautious and careful to follow the prescribed safeguards mentioned previously.

Evangelists often limit their dating to individuals apart from the congregations in which they are ministering, and they often refrain from any dating during active revival meetings. Further, pastors often request or require that evangelists refrain from dating during revivals and are especially reluctant to allow the evangelist to date members of his or her congregation, at least during that particular time. These practices and disciplines highlight the concerns that dating causes to arise. Evangelists cannot be too careful concerning their conduct toward those of the opposite sex. They are human and temptations can arise unexpectedly. But beyond that, their reputations can suffer irreparable damage even from innocent conduct when they allow themselves to enter into a questionable situation or relationship. It is vital that they rigorously limit their dating while ministering as an evangelist.

Counseling. Perhaps single ministers may not become involved in counseling as often as married ministers do, but it is possible. For instance, consider an unmarried pastor. That pastor may have entered into a pastorate as a single person or it is possible the pastor has suffered the loss of a companion and is suddenly single. Whatever the case, that single pastor probably will have congregants seeking pastoral advice and counsel. He or she must exercise great care in giving counsel.

Sometimes there are Apostolic counselors in the area who are specifically credentialed for counseling, which can be a great option for a single pastor. Still, there may be those moments before or after church services in which a person is just seeking out the wisdom of his or her pastor. Here are a couple of practices many have used to safeguard themselves in such circumstances:

1. Some ministers counsel laity in the auditorium on the platform or possibly in the altar area. Many pastors have found this approach helpful for many reasons, but it is especially beneficial when needing to meet with members of the opposite sex regardless of the person's married status.

2. If meeting in an office, either the door should be kept open or there should be a large window through which others can see you at all times, which keeps the two in session from having visual privacy. Clearly, many topics require confidentiality, which may cause a pastor to close a door for privacy. Still, the two should never be out of sight visually. Further, these guidelines are presuming the office is in a high-traffic area of the church. If the office is remotely located or away from busy and active areas, the pastor simply cannot afford to risk meeting with the other-sex church member in his or her office. Pastors must keep the very highest standards and protocols in mind at all times, which is for the benefit and protection of not only themselves, but also of those with whom they may meet.

MARRIED MINISTERS
Whether married or not, many of the same concerns and responsibilities exist for all ministers. Married evangelists and pastors also must be cognizant of their high moral responsibilities. They must think ahead to avoid situations in

which Satan would love to entrap them. He takes great delight in causing ministers to have to deal with the pressure cooker of temptation, sometimes spoiling their sterling reputation and sometimes destroying their ability to minister effectively to others.

One of the significant areas of temptation for married ministers involves necessary times of separation due to ministry or other work commitments. A minister might be an itinerant evangelist involved in ministry that requires travel but with a spouse who is unable to travel due to responsibilities at home. These kinds of mutually agreed upon periods of separation can work, but only when both partners are willing to work with the dynamics short-term separations create.

There are practical considerations in such cases that must be thought through. Who will be responsible for keeping bills paid? Who will care for the maintenance around the home? How often will the partners be able to spend quality time together and where will they spend that time? What about the sexual needs of the partners? Lengthy separations from one's spouse can open up married individuals to temptation. Paul addressed such separations.

"Do not deprive one another except with consent for a time, that you may give yourselves to fasting and prayer; and come together again so that Satan does not tempt you because of your lack of self-control" (I Corinthians 7:5, NKJV). God knows that separations that deprive married companions of their normal, healthy times of sexual fulfilment open wide the door to sexual temptation. Either or both of the two companions could succumb to temptation, falter in their resolve, and fall into unfaithfulness and sexual sin. Married ministers should recognize in advance the challenges and dangers of temporary separations, and both companions should be willing and prepared to confront those challenges in a positive and victorious fashion.

We live in a secularized culture that questions the need for taking so many ethical precautions to protect our integrity. The culture suggests, "We are adults. It is no one else's business the decisions we make and the lives we lead."

To the culture's objections we would simply respond, treasures are worth expending great effort in order to protect them. Our moral integrity and our godly reputation are treasures. We should do all we can to protect these treasures from the encroachment of a godless culture driven by the evil influences of satanic forces. One would only need to ask a person who has suffered the loss of integrity through moral failure to learn of the intense pain caused by such loss. It is tragic when moral failure occurs, and we should do everything possible to avoid it. Still, there is hope and help for those who have fallen to temptation and into the pit of immorality.

THE PROBLEM OF AND RECOVERY FROM MORAL FAILURE

The writer of Proverbs observed, "A good name is rather to be chosen than great riches, and loving favour rather than silver and gold" (Proverbs 22:1). Riches can be regained, but it is virtually impossible to recover a "good name" once lost. Repairing it is terribly painful and excruciatingly difficult.

The pain and suffering caused by moral failure is indescribable. It is a wretched, tormenting agony for the innocent parties who suffer from another's descent into immorality, but it also is a source of intense suffering for the guilty ones. One momentary lapse of judgment, a succumbing to unexpected temptation, and the guilty person is set to suffer immeasurably and possibly so for the rest of his or her life. Further, take this pain and multiply it tenfold, and you are possibly approaching the miserable suffering moral failure causes for a minister of the gospel of Jesus Christ.

Not only do ministers who fall into moral failure lose their good name and suffer the repercussions of immorality, they also lose the opportunities of effective ministry and the livelihood they received through ministry. They suddenly land in a lonely place without a pulpit to preach in, without a ministry to influence people for Christ, and without an income. It is a devastating loss!

Still, as horrible as the pit of moral failure may be, not all is irreparably lost. The minister can be restored to salvation and relationship with Jesus Christ. Moral failure will unquestionably leave the marks of its taunting tentacles in a person's life and it might never be possible to recover a ministry, but the grace of God ensures that redemption is possible.

The high cost of moral failure is hard to comprehend, but the strength of the grace of God is unmatched in its ability to redeem the hopeless and helpless. The minister can find forgiveness and salvation in the arms of Jesus.

CONCLUSION

This chapter has attempted to encourage and guide all individuals to avoid temptation or problematic situations in their interactions with those of the opposite sex. Whether single or married, men or women, laypersons or ministers— all believers should safeguard their integrity and reputation with zealous caution and determination for maintaining right relationships. Men and women alike have to recognize the precarious pitfalls surrounding their relationships with those of the opposite sex, some of which have the potential to devastate their lives and destroy their reputations.

Perhaps some individuals may conclude that not all of the advice given in this chapter is essential. A person might say, "I'm a responsible adult Christian who loves God. I am not going to fall into moral sin. I will be just fine." And it is certainly plausible they might be OK and never suffer the loss of their reputation, community standing, or ministry. However, is our relationship with Jesus Christ not worth taking the extra precautions to protect it? Is our reputation as a Christian believer or minister of so little value to us that we would take chances by being careless in how we interact with members of the opposite sex? For me personally, I am unwilling to take that risk. I value too greatly what God has given to me. Further, I have a wife, three daughters, and many grandchildren who are looking to me and the life I live in Christ Jesus.

I believe I will choose the pathway of ethical integrity and do my best to take no risks in how I interact with others—especially others of the opposite sex who are not my wife and family.

CHAPTER EIGHT

AVOIDING THE
TRAP OF CRITICISM

A friend of mine once said, "What you are not 'up on,' you are usually 'down on.'" How easy it is to criticize things about which we know little or nothing, or things we do not understand!

The words critical, criticism, and discrediting are not in the Bible, but the ideas they portray are there. These ideas are expressed through words such as "slanderously," "blaspheme," "speak evil of," "rail on," and "revile." These words (in the KJV) are translated from the Greek word *blasphemeo*. *Enhanced Strong's Dictionary* defines the word *blasphemeo* as "to vilify; specially, to speak impiously: KJV — (speak) blaspheme (-er, -mously, -my), defame, rail on, revile, speak evil."

Another Greek word in the New Testament that gives the same basic idea is *katalaleo,* which *Strong's Concordance* defines as "to be a traducer, i.e. to slander: KJV — speak against (evil of)." An occurrence of this word is found in James 4:11–12: "Speak not evil one of another, brethren. He that speaketh evil of his brother, and judgeth his brother, speaketh evil of the law, and judgeth the law: but if thou judge the law, thou art not a doer of the law, but a judge. There is one lawgiver, who is able to save and to destroy: who art thou that judgest another?"

ARE WE TO JUDGE OTHERS?

The word "judge" is translated from the Greek word *krino*, which means "properly, to distinguish, i.e. decide (mentally or judicially); by implication, to try, condemn, punish: — avenge, conclude, condemn, damn, decree, determine, esteem, judge, go to (sue at the) law, ordain, call in question, sentence to, think" (*Enhanced Strong's Dictionary*).

Jesus strongly condemned judging others lest we be judged by the same measurement (Matthew 7:1–2). We should consider carefully His teachings on the matter and what our duty is as Christians.

Judging Others

> Judge not, that ye be not judged. For with what judgment ye judge, ye shall be judged: and with what measure ye mete, it shall be measured to you again. (Matthew 7:1–2)

> Therefore thou art inexcusable, O man, whosoever thou art that judgest: for wherein thou judgest another, thou condemnest thyself; for thou that judgest doest the same things. But we are sure that the judgment of God is according to truth against

> them which commit such things. And thinkest
> thou this, O man, that judgest them which do such
> things, and doest the same, that thou shalt escape
> the judgment of God? . . . Who will render to every
> man according to his deeds. (Romans 2:1–6)

Clearly, both Jesus and Paul taught against judging others. However, many individuals in our contemporary culture have made their condemnation of judgment broader and more encompassing than either Jesus or Paul ever intended. Many people want impunity for their evil conduct while they cry, "Don't judge me! Don't judge me!" They have taken some statements from Scripture and misapplied them. In the process, they have intimidated many well-intentioned Christians into believing no judgment whatsoever is allowed, which is not the case.

As revealed by the definitions of the Greek words, there are different aspects of judgment. We are to avoid making some judgments, yet others the Scriptures command us to make. How do we distinguish between the two? We could narrow and condense the concept of judgment to the following two basic categories:

- To Discern, Distinguish, Determine, or Decide;
- To Condemn or Punish.

When viewing these two basic categories of judgment, it is clear the two are quite different in both their results and in the attitude behind them. Let us consider first the idea of discernment or determination.

Making Judgments of Discernment or Determination
A careful examination of the Scriptures reveals we do make certain judgments, but they are not to involve the condemnation, slandering, or discrediting of others. Rather, they involve personal discernment or distinguishing certain things about other individuals or situations.

Jesus once presented an illustration of two debtors whose debts were dismissed. He asked the disciples which forgiven debtor would most love the master who had forgiven the debts. When Simon answered it would probably be the one "to whom he forgave most," Jesus responded, "Thou hast rightly judged" (Luke 7:43). According to Jesus Christ, there is such a thing as correct judgment—not all judgment is taboo. Again, in Luke 12:56–57 Jesus spoke of judgment in a positive and necessary way. Further, he compared some judgment (verse 57) with the ability to discern (verse 56). In John 7:24 Jesus referred to what He called "righteous judgment."

There are aspects of judgment that are both right to make and even necessary. It is good to discern or judge some situations and make decisions or determinations based on that judgment. In Acts 20:16, Luke the writer made a reference to Paul making a determination to sail by Ephesus. In this verse Luke used the same Greek word, *krino*, which often is translated as a form of judge or judgment. The verse states, "For Paul had determined to sail by Ephesus" (Acts 20:16). In other words, Paul made a judgment call—a discernment or determination—as to what actions he would take. It is a judgment we all must make often in our lives.

Other examples of this same usage include Acts 25:25 and Acts 27:1.

We make judgments or determinations of this nature every day. We decide what we will have for breakfast or which route to take when driving from one place to another. We decide whether it will be best to have a birthday party on Friday night or Saturday morning. These are judgments and they are not wrong.

Further, the Scriptures even command us to make some judgments: "Beloved, believe not every spirit, but try the spirits whether they are of God: because many false prophets are gone out into the world" (I John 4:1). We have to "try the spirits," which is judging what kind of spirits they are—whether or not they are of God. This involves personal discernment (although usually prompted by the Holy Spirit) or judgment, which we must make. It is vital for believers to judge the spirits around them.

Judgments That Condemn or Punish

If we are to discern spirits and make certain personal judgments, what kind of judgment has the Scriptures condemned? It is unacceptable for us to make judgments of condemnation against others. We may discern that a person's spirit is wrong—and that discernment may guide our cautious interactions with that person. Still, it is not our place to condemn the individual, unless the legal system has made us a judge for the maintenance of a lawful society. Black-robed judges have the job and civic responsibility of making legal determinations, but most of us do not.

We cannot see or know a person's heart. Only God knows those things about an individual. It is not our place to condemn, but to love and to pray for others. We leave judgment that condemns in the hands of lawful judges, and the ultimate judgment to the only true and righteous Judge.

The Righteous Judge

God is the only righteous judge. He alone is truly righteous and able to discern fully between right and wrong. That is the reason Paul strongly condemned individuals taking actions of vengeance. Vengeance belongs to God alone (Romans 12:19). (See also Deuteronomy 32:35; Psalm 94:1; Hebrews 10:30; I Thessalonians 4:6.)

One minister told about preaching a funeral for a scoundrel. He read the Scripture verse, "For we must all appear before the judgment seat of Christ" (II Corinthians 5:10). Then he told the family and friends, "This man is blessed. He will stand before the only righteous Judge. I am not his judge. You are not his judge. God is, and for that reason this man is blessed."

Paul in his second letter to Timothy called the Lord "the righteous judge" (II Timothy 4:8). Further, there are Scriptures throughout the Bible that characterize the Lord's judgments as being righteous: Psalm 119:7, 62, 106, 160, 164; Romans 2:5; II Thessalonians 1:5. In Abraham's pleading with God on behalf of the people of Sodom and Gomorrah, it is clear Abraham expected God would exercise judgment righteously:

> That be far from thee to do after this manner, to slay the righteous with the wicked: and that the righteous should be as the wicked, that be far from thee: Shall not the Judge of all the earth do right? (Genesis 18:25)

God is righteous, fair, and impartial, and He judges according to righteousness and truth. His judgments are altogether "true and righteous" (Revelation 16:7). (See also Psalm 96:13; Romans 2:2.) It is sobering that God will judge all individuals, but we have confidence in His fairness, love, and mercy, which govern His divine judgment.

What are the basic principles that should govern our ethical conduct in the matter of our perception of others?

The Right Spirit
What is most important for a believer is that his or her spirit and attitude is right—not judgmental, critical, or condemning.

DO NOT SPEAK EVIL OF OTHERS
It is both presumptuous and wrong for believers to speak evil of the thoughts, motives, or actions of others. (See Titus 3:2.) It is impossible for us to know another person's thoughts or motives. We may recognize unacceptable conduct in others, and we do make certain discernments or judgments about such behavior. Still, we have no authorization or right to condemn them. The Lord is the Righteous Judge; He alone will correct their conduct, ultimately.

The believer's responsibility is to approach the matter with kindness, gentleness, humility, and mercy. After all, who among us has not made mistakes and suffered lapses in judgment? We all have done wrong, but the Lord was gracious and kind to forgive us, and our concern for all individuals is that they be saved. To Titus, Paul wrote, "For we ourselves also were sometimes foolish, disobedient, deceived, serving divers lusts and pleasures, living in malice and envy, hateful, and hating one another. But after that the kindness and love of God our

Saviour toward man appeared, not by works of righteousness which we have done, but according to his mercy he saved us, by the washing of regeneration, and renewing of the Holy Ghost" (Titus 3:3–5).

Clearly, we should avoid speaking evil of others because the Scriptures condemn it. However, perhaps we can identify some additional reasons for refraining from criticizing others.

(1) First, we should refrain from such criticism because it is unkind and offensive. A person might protest that it was the other individual's actions that were the first to cause offense. But that gives an individual no right or license to mimic their conduct and engage in a war of unkind words. Jesus warned against offending His children in Mark 9:37–42: "Whosoever shall receive one of such children in my name, receiveth me. . . . And whosoever shall offend one of these little ones that believe in me, it is better for him that a millstone were hanged about his neck, and he were cast into the sea."

One could also argue that the offender was not a child, only acting like one. That may be true, but Jesus said we all have to become like children to enter the kingdom of Heaven (Matthew 18:3). It would seem logical that He not only cares deeply about children, but also about adults. Further, perhaps a person is still immature in his relationship with Jesus Christ.

It only makes sense that we would love all people regardless of age and try to avoid being offensive. Even if we genuinely believe ourselves to be in the right, we should not intentionally offend others.

(2) It is impossible for us to know all the facts, and we can never know the motives and intents of another person's actions. Who are we to judge them? We question their behavior and our concerns may affect how we interact with them. For

example, their actions might limit our ability to develop a close relationship with them. But we still should love them, be kind to them, and pray for them. We are to pray even for those who hurt us terribly. Jesus said, "Love your enemies, bless them that curse you, do good to them that hate you, and pray for them which despitefully use you, and persecute you" (Matthew 5:44).

The Sin of Presumption

Merriam-Webster Dictionary gives a primary definition of *presumption* as "a belief that something is true even though it has not been proved." Too many people—even believers—are too quick to believe the negative reports they hear about others and too slow to believe the good reports. Consequently, they sometimes become guilty of spreading rumors and innuendo, which hurt the other person's reputation whether or not the rumor is even true. This behavior is gossip and it also is an aspect of "evil speaking." Frankly, it is a sin.

Peter made the seriousness of this sin quite clear in his second epistle.

> The Lord knoweth how to deliver the godly out of temptations, and to reserve the unjust unto the day of judgment to be punished: but chiefly them that walk after the flesh in the lust of uncleanness, and despise government. Presumptuous are they, selfwilled, they are not afraid to speak evil of dignities. Whereas angels, which are greater in power and might, bring not railing accusation against them before the Lord. But these, as natural brute beasts, made to be taken and destroyed,

> speak evil of the things that they understand not;
> and shall utterly perish in their own corruption;
> and shall receive the reward of unrighteousness, as
> they that count it pleasure to riot in the day time.
> Spots they are and blemishes, sporting themselves
> with their own deceivings while they feast with
> you. (II Peter 2:9–22)

(See also Jude 8–12.)

What is it about human nature that wants to believe the worst about people? We ought to give people the benefit of every doubt, love them, and pray for them. What we have heard may not be true, but if it is true, our ethical responsibility is to love them and pray for them. Love does not motivate us to spread evil or negative reports. Love compels us to be kind and prayerful. Prayer is the best thing we could do for them.

Gossip and evil speaking are a spiritual disease. They are contagious and deadly. We need to run from them with all our strength. And these two rabid, infectious modes of conduct have a related behavior that also is contagious: murmuring and complaining.

The Spirit of Murmuring and Complaining

Murmuring and complaining are driven by an evil spirit, and it is contagious! That does not suggest a complainer is demon possessed, although he or she might be. It means these behaviors reflect an infected attitude that performs the work of the evil one on a person's behalf. When we succumb to this line of conduct, we are influenced by Satan and we are doing his work. When we spread rumors, bear tales about others, or complain incessantly, we are modeling one of the other names for Satan: "Accuser of our brethren" (Revelation 12:10).

The devil accuses and complains against believers in Jesus Christ. He continually tries to tear them down, inhibit them, and destroy them—never to build them up, improve their life, assist them, or comfort them. In fact, Abaddon or Destroyer is yet another name for the devil (Revelation 9:11).

Too often we see the accuser's work and influence among individuals associated with the church. He continually tries to plant seeds of discontentment in believers, causing them to be unhappy or confused. He seems to love watching those who suffer from discontentment as they complain about everything in the church. It may be about the sound system, the temperature, or someone else occupying their favorite place to sit. Anything and everything—they will find a way to complain and murmur to all who will listen. Their behavior is not only unethical in their treatment toward the body of Christ and the church leadership, but their conduct is sinful. We need to learn to be content—or at least not to complain when we are dissatisfied about things.

Paul told the Philippian believers he had "learned . . . to be content" no matter what situation came his way (Philippians 4:11). Contentment is not a matter of having everything as we like it to be. Contentment is a decision—a decision to accept our circumstances as they come and to look for the good God will bring out of them.

Sadly, some people are whiners. They never seem to be happy unless they are complaining about something.

1. Consider Israel in the Wilderness. The Israelites in the Old Testament exodus complained and complained and complained. It seemed nothing satisfied them and they constantly railed against the leadership of Moses. (See Exodus 15:24; 16:2, 7–12; 17:3; Numbers 14:2, 27–36. These are only a handful of the many instances of the Israelites' complaining.) The complaining and murmuring of the Israelites seemed never to cease. Whenever the Lord would respond to their complaint and supply a need, they always seemed to find something else to complain about.

> I have heard the murmurings of the children of Israel: speak unto them, saying, At even ye shall eat flesh, and in the morning ye shall be filled with bread; and ye shall know that I am the LORD your God. And it came to pass, that at even the quails came up, and covered the camp: and in the morning the dew lay round about the host. And when the dew that lay was gone up, behold, upon the face of the wilderness there lay a small round thing, as small as the hoar frost on the ground. And when the children of Israel saw it, they said one to another, It is manna: for they wist not what it was. And Moses said unto them, This is the bread which the LORD hath given you to eat. (Exodus 16:12–15)

God gave the Israelites manna and quail to eat, but even still they became dissatisfied and complained. (See Numbers 11:6.) God and Moses became angry with the people for their constant murmuring, and the Lord sent them so much quail they became sick of them. (See Numbers 11.) God judged them for their complaining spirit and sent a plague among them causing many to die (Numbers 11:33–34).

2. Christians in Local Assemblies. One would think believers would read the Old Testament stories of Israel and learn from the mistakes of the Jews' complaining and murmuring. Unfortunately, some people never seem to learn, and there never seems to be a shortage of complainers in the local church. It is sad. We have much for which to be grateful, but some people choose rather to murmur about the things they dislike.

When a person continually complains, that person builds a habit of complaining. Sometimes he or she may not even realize they have developed such a habit because it has become commonplace and second nature to the person. This is dangerous because the individual is falling into the trap of criticism. Before you know it, he or she is consumed by a critical spirit or attitude and murmurs and complains constantly.

Individuals with a critical attitude may even go so far as to become slanderous in their criticisms of church leadership or fellow believers. They discredit their fellow believers and sometimes harm the reputations of others. It is indeed a serious and dangerous disease and we must avoid it at all costs. It is unethical to live with continual complaining and murmuring against others in the body of Christ. When we complain against others in the church, we are making a grave error that is twofold: (1) we are complaining against ourselves for we too are a member of Christ's body; (2) we actually are complaining against the Lord Himself because the church is His body on earth.

Let us turn from our critical spirits and complaining ways and learn to be kind, supportive, and prayerful over things that concern us. May God deliver us from having a critical spirit and may we truly learn to be grateful for all of His blessings.

CHAPTER NINE

LIVING AS A SPIRITUAL LEADER

If we desire to live in this world as individuals who possess the highest standards of ethics, we must learn to live as spiritual leaders. We should desire to stand out as positive examples of Christian conduct and spirituality.

Phil Stevenson observed, "It is through the regular and consistent development of a relationship with God that leadership is enhanced. Neglecting spiritual growth will stunt our leadership. Leaders tend to focus on *doing* things. We plan events, strategize, make and keep appointments, and prepare lessons. None of this is wrong—unless the leader is not taking time to make the necessary spiritual deposits" (Phil Stevenson, *5 Things Anyone Can Do to Lead Effectively*, You Can! [Indianapolis, IN: WPH, 2007], 79).

One might be tempted to say, "But wait! I'm not a leader; I'm a layperson." Everyone leads someone. Somebody is looking to each of us on some level. They watch our conduct and observe our ideals—or lack thereof—and they are poised to model and emulate us in their behavior. To that person—or possibly many individuals—we are leaders. We ought to consider living in a way worthy of emulation and modeling.

Boil Christian ethics down to its most basic essence. Simply, it would be living in relationship with God, doing what pleases Him, and living in relationship and harmony with others. If one were to focus on those three considerations about life, the person surely would live in biblically ethical purity.

LIVING IN RELATIONSHIP WITH GOD

Theoretically, a person could be fundamentally ethical without being a Christian. However, as discussed early in this book, the basic laws and principles of morality have their roots in the Scriptures. Many principles of Christianity are necessarily inseparable components of ethics. The most important element of Christian ethics is a person's relationship with Jesus Christ.

Pure Christian ethics require a foundation of relationship with Jesus Christ. If a person demonstrates he or she is ethically challenged, his or her conduct belies the person's relationship with Christ. Something is wrong with our relationship with God if we are incapable of or negligent in demonstrating honest, ethical behavior.

Relationship with Christ flows out of one being filled with His Holy Spirit and proceeding to walk with Him. The faithful exercise of spiritual disciplines nurtures and enhances our relationship with Christ. Prayer, fasting, regular church attendance and fellowship, Bible reading and study, and meditating on the Lord—all these disciplines build us up in Christ. Further, these disciplines stimulate consistent spiritual growth.

As a person grows in relationship with Jesus Christ, he or she becomes increasingly aware of the things that please or displease the Lord. The person grows in his or her desire to avoid doing things that displease God. He or she fervently wants to please the Lord in every aspect of life.

DOING WHAT PLEASES GOD

What a delight it is to please someone we love dearly, whether a spouse, a parent, a child, or a special friend! It is pleasurable to recognize that our actions have connected in a special way and made that individual happy. In a similar way, it is a sheer delight to bring special pleasure to God and live within the aura of divine favor.

As a Christian grows in the faith and recognizes what honors and pleases God, he or she grows in the Lord's favor and in relationship with Him. The believer grows spiritually and becomes a leader to others. This is what we call living as a spiritual leader.

Something interesting happens as a person is developing in relationship with Jesus Christ and endeavoring to do all that pleases Him. That person also grows in his or her relationship with fellow believers.

LIVING IN RELATIONSHIP
AND HARMONY WITH OTHERS

John Donne wrote the poem "No Man Is an Island." He wrote, "No man is an island, entire of itself, every man is a piece of the continent, a part of the main." In no area of human life is this truer than in the church of the Lord Jesus Christ. The church is the body of Christ on earth with every individual member separate but yet part of the unified whole. Each member has his or her own place and function within the body, but all members function together toward the operation of the entire body.

> For as we have many members in one body, and all members have not the same office: so we, being many, are one body in Christ, and every one members one of another. (Romans 12:4–5)

> (See also I Corinthians 12:12–27.)

It makes no sense for a person to desire disharmony within his or her own human body, which is what we call disease. No one wants to be sick or suffer a surgery requiring the removal of a hand or foot or body organ. Why then would we tolerate disharmony in the body of Christ, the church?

Every sincere believer will naturally work toward harmony within the church as he or she matures in spiritual leadership. The Christian strives to please the Lord in all things, but he or she also works to enjoy spiritual harmony with fellow believers.

What contributes to harmony within Christ's body?

- Corporate prayer and worship
- Fellowship
- Christian ethics

As believers treat one another as they themselves desire to be treated, appreciation for one another grows and multiplies. The natural love members of Christ's body have for one another grows, and mutual respect and warmth grow exponentially. If there is one thing above other things that will work against harmony and Christian fellowship, it is the lack of ethical conduct. Unethical behavior creates animosity, resentment, and disharmony. That is a major reason to focus on truly caring for fellow Christians and treating others with the utmost ethical considerations.

CHAPTER TEN

ETHICS
OF INFLUENCE

The media delights in flaunting the moral failings of powerful, influential people. Christian ethics requires an individual to consider carefully the great responsibility of properly handling his or her power and influence with others.

Sadly, we live in a wicked time that has witnessed great moral failings among individuals of remarkable power and influence. A few recent examples are as follows:

- Sexual abuse of young subordinates by Roman Catholic priests and the consequent cover-up of those abuses by some Catholic officials.
- The second impeachment in US history of a president, that of President William Jefferson Clinton, for lying under oath and obstructing justice. Although the US

Senate did not vote to remove Clinton from office, his impeachment nevertheless tainted his record. The impeachment was for dishonesty in dealing with a federal grand jury, but possibly even more serious was that he abused his power of influence with a young intern. Even in situations of consensual sexual involvement, the older person who possesses great power and influence bears an enormous responsibility toward the younger, more impressionable party. In addition to one's ethical responsibilities to those within his or her influence, the person has moral obligations.

- Numerous teachers charged and tried for having sexual encounters with their students, which is a clear-cut abuse of power and influence.

It is a serious matter when a person of influence uses that influence to coerce or entice a subordinate into misbehavior or inappropriate conduct. Whether sexual, criminal, or merely questionable behavior, influential individuals should never draw others into misconduct. Such conduct is an abusive use of influence.

Influence is a sacred trust a leader must handle with great care and caution. It is wrong to lead another individual astray through the exercise of one's influence or power.

EXAMPLES OF INFLUENTIAL PEOPLE

Any person may assume a position in which he or she is vested with power and influence. This is especially true of some supervisors, managers, or bosses. Some positions possess great influence because of the nature of the work or position itself. For instance, consider the following positions:

- *Boss over His or Her Employees.* Employees often have a natural fear of their bosses or supervisors. They rely on the wages earned on their job for their livelihood. Often, they live within such tight budgets that if they were to lose their job, they may be able to manage their expenses for only a few weeks. And if they were to lose their job, they realize it may be difficult to find another job and replace their income in a timely fashion. All these concerns considered, they fear their boss and his or her ability to terminate their employment. This natural fear empowers the boss with enormous influence. The boss can and should exercise that influence carefully for the betterment of both the company and the employee. When influence is wielded maliciously or deviously, the boss also has the opportunity to force or pressure the employee into inappropriate conduct. This is the abusive use of influence.
- *Police Officers.* A police officer has authority, power, and influence. The officer can utilize that influence in a positive fashion within a community, but is also capable of abusing his or her influence. A police officer can use influence to lead the youth toward positive activities in the community, or can abuse that influence to gain various favors from victims. Their presence also often evokes fear, which again opens the door to possible abuses should one be inclined to take advantage of another individual. Thankfully, many police officers are honest, decent public servants who are an asset to a community. But it is vital they bear in mind the power of their influence and that they use their influence judiciously and for the positive good.

Consider the impact one police officer, Bobby White, made on some boys playing basketball in Gainesville, Florida. Answering a complaint call about the noise, White ended up playing ball with the boys. According to an article on www.nbazone. xyz, "The footage of Officer White's interaction with the kids soon went viral and was watched by millions including Shaquille O'Neal. Touched by Officer White's actions, the basketball legend paid a visit to the Gainesville Police Department.... Subsequently, O'Neal, Officer White, and other officers decided to go see the same kids." These men made a profoundly positive impact on some boys playing basketball in the street. They demonstrated how to use one's influence for good.

- *Ministers.* Ministers of the gospel are certainly individuals of influence. They bear an enormous responsibility to lead people to Jesus Christ and not to abuse them. Along with what has happened among priests, there also have been ministers in Protestant churches who have abused their influence and authority to gain favors, especially sexual. Again, most ministers are good and godly citizens whether or not they preach the Apostolic message. They are generally a blessing to the community and a positive force for good. They all possess great influence and power, and they must exercise it with extreme caution. It is wrong to abuse people whether that abuse is spiritual, physical, sexual, mental, or emotional. All abuse is wrong and when it is perpetrated by individuals of influence, the sin bears even more reproach, shame, and guilt.

- *Teachers.* A teacher has much influence within his or her classroom. Students want to be well liked and are susceptible to subtle abuses plied against them. Also, students want to make good grades and enjoy a special status within the classroom. These desires coupled with their natural admiration of their teachers place incredible power and influence into the hands of a teacher. The teachers are responsible and accountable for how they handle that influence. If they use their influence to take advantage of a student, they will be held accountable by society, and ultimately, by God. If they use their influence to guide students in their quest for education, they will be honored, recognized, praised, and appreciated. Most of all, they will have the satisfaction of knowing they have done their job well and maintained their integrity before God.

- *Individuals in Elected Governmental Positions.* People who are elected to various positions of government—secular or spiritual—often are viewed with great admiration and respect. Dishonest and unethical officials have the opportunity to take advantage of that and abuse their position to gain influence over their victims. They have a higher obligation of responsibility to use their influence judiciously for the public good, and never to heap selfish benefit upon themselves.

In February 2016, several elected officials in the small town of Crystal City, Texas, were arrested. According to the Huffington Post, the officials were "accused of accepting thousands of dollars in bribes and helping an illegal gambling operation. . . . The federal indictment alleges . . . the city's officials used their positions 'to enrich themselves by soliciting and accepting bribes'" ("Almost All The Top Officials In This Texas Town Were Arrested For Corruption," Matt Ferner, accessed July 2, 2016).

Where the word of a king is, there is power: and who may say unto him, What doest thou? (Ecclesiastes 8:4)

It is possible for anyone to take advantage of other individuals under his or her authority, power, or influence. However, the individuals mentioned above are particularly susceptible to the temptation to wield their influence abusively. They must exercise great care and ethical purity to avoid the temptation to abuse those who are vulnerable. One thing is certain: temptation will reveal those who operate with high ethics and those who unethically take advantage of others for selfish gain.

CHAPTER ELEVEN

ETHICS IN THE WORKPLACE

Ethics within the workplace is an important topic. The continual interactions between employees and management, as well as the constant engagements between coworkers are greatly enhanced through appropriate and ethical conduct. When the corporate culture of any business or organization cultivates and encourages high ethics, it is a tremendous asset to that entity and to every employee. Ethics is vital on the job!

OFFICE POLITICS
"'Office politics' are the strategies that people play to gain advantage, personally or for a cause they support. The term often has a negative connotation, in that it refers to strategies people use to seek advantage at the expense of others or the greater good. In this context, it often adversely affects the

working environment and relationships within it" (www. mindtools.com, "Dealing With Office Politics," accessed June 21, 2016).

Because of the fallen human nature, office politics show up at virtually every workplace, every organization, or every group where numerous people undertake a cooperative effort. The attitudes and activities generated by office politics include many things that should have no place in a Christian's life, such as gossip, backbiting, critical attitudes, and cliques. These attitudes and other similar ones do not reflect Christian ethics, values, or conduct, but Christians will encounter them in many workplaces.

Christians should distance themselves from negative office politics. They should be known throughout the workplace as individuals you can confide in who will not break confidence. They should be the ones coworkers turn to when needing prayer or counsel. They should be stabilizing sources of strength and dependability within the company or organization.

It is not easy to ignore criticisms and ugly gossip about us, which hurt and are demoralizing. Still, that is the best and most ethical course of action. Christians should take their painful concerns to the Lord in prayer and trust Him to rectify the situation. Perhaps the Lord can use these Christians as encouragers in the face of antagonizing gutter politics. The Lord has a way of turning all negative experiences into positives on behalf of those who keep their trust anchored securely in Him. (See Romans 8:28.)

HONESTY

Christians should be known as the most trustworthy, honest employees in a company or organization. They should be the ones the managers turn to when needing trustworthy individuals for delicate assignments, such as keeping confidential files. They may be entrusted with the safekeeping of monies or other valuables. They should be the kind of employees managers are happy to have, especially when they need reliable and responsible individuals to care for important duties.

Too many employees think nothing of taking office supplies home without approval for their own personal use. Some employees even joke about all they are "stealing" from the office. Some individuals easily justify their dishonest conduct on the basis of not being paid the salary they believe they are due. A few even cross the line of criminality by embezzling money from the company. Whether it is something small in value or priceless, it is wrong to steal or take that which does not belong to us. Dishonesty has no place within the ethical practices of a Christian.

An employee may need supplies for work he or she is doing for the company from home during after-hours. In such cases, it is always best to seek prior approval for allocating supplies for use at home. Even if one is sure the boss will not mind, it is always advisable to take the highest ethical approach by asking. Taking that approach will further bolster the employer's opinion of the employee and his or her confidence in the employee's ethics.

Trust is important in business and work relationships. The employer needs to have confidence in those who work there. However, the employees also should have confidence in those who manage, supervise, and own the company. Mutual trust and confidence are indispensable in the workplace, which calls for Christians to maintain only the highest possible ethical practices.

Being a writer, I must address another aspect of honest ethics in the workplace, although it may be a different kind of business. I am referring to honesty in writing—avoiding plagiarism. I could have addressed this topic in many of the chapters of this book, but I decided to tackle it from the perspective of one's work.

It is dishonest to copy the work of another person and take credit for it as if it were one's own. *The Merriam-Webster Dictionary* defines *plagiarism* as "the act of using another person's words or ideas without giving credit to that person."

I recall an unfortunate situation in the 1980s while serving on the Executive Publication Committee of the United Pentecostal Church. We accepted a book at that time in which we discovered—unfortunately, after publication—a severe case of plagiarism. We went through the book, comparing it line by line with a previous work published outside the UPCI. Entire pages and sometimes entire chapters were copied almost word for word. We had no choice but to discontinue sales, pull the printed inventory of the book from the shelves, and destroy them. One person's dishonesty cost the publishing house thousands of dollars.

It is stealing to take another person's intellectual property and pawn it off as your own. There are rigid copyright laws that govern how another person's words can and cannot be used. Credit must be given to the author, and even the use of credited quotations are governed and limited by law.

Whether writing articles and books for publication or writing research papers for school assignments, it is only ethical to give credit where credit is due. Use your own words for the most part and provide only limited, credited quotations as appropriate.

KEEPING COMMITMENTS

In years gone by there was a saying often heard, "My word is my bond." Although the saying is seldom heard now, *Cambridge Dictionary and Thesaurus* defines "*Your word is your bond*" as "(old-fashioned or formal) If someone's word is their bond, they always keep a promise: 'But listen, you have to promise never to tell anyone.' 'My word is my bond'" (*Cambridge Advanced Learners Dictionary & Thesaurus*, Cambridge University Press).

When a Christian gives his word on a matter, others should be able to have complete confidence it is true to the best of his or her knowledge. If the employee makes a commitment to his or her boss, the employer should know it will be done as promised. It may be a commitment to get a project completed, to come into work for overtime, or to cover for another employee. Whatever it involves, a Christian's word should be reliable, trustworthy, and believable.

We should say what we mean and mean what we say. Too many people are quick to volunteer for extra assignments or responsibilities, but when the time comes for them to fulfill their commitment they are nowhere to be found. It is frustrating to be waiting on someone to show up—someone who made a commitment to be there at a certain time—but the person never shows up. We should keep commitments made to our employer, employee, or coworkers. It is the ethical thing to do.

Christian ethics requires us to keep our promises and commitments to the best of our ability. If something unforeseen comes up that keeps us from fulfilling our commitment, we owe a timely notification, explanation, and apology to the one to whom we made the commitment. That is ethical conduct.

DEPENDABILITY

Ability is a great asset, but dependability is even greater. It is one thing to have great ability to perform the tasks our work requires, but that ability is only as valuable as our faithfulness. It is worthless if we fail to show up when expected and perform as needed. The employer is depending on the employee. He or she should have a reputation for dependability. The employer should know he or she can count on the believer to keep his or her word. The employee should be on the job as expected and fulfill the assigned duties as anticipated.

This principle may seem to apply less toward the employer, but the boss and the company should be dependable as well. Whatever commitments have been made to the employees, the employers should keep them as expected. If the company wants and expects its employees to exhibit dependability, management also must demonstrate dependability.

FAIRNESS

An employer should keep his commitments and be fair to his employees who enable the company to function and make a profit. It is wrong to take advantage of those who are poor and needy, or financially struggling. The worker is worthy of his hire (Luke 10:7). Give the employee an honest day's wage for his work. Be thoughtful, kind, and fair in dealing with the employee and his or her needs.

> Thou shalt not oppress an hired servant that is poor and needy, whether he be of thy brethren, or of thy strangers that are in thy land within thy gates: at his day thou shalt give him his hire, neither shall the sun go down upon it; for he is poor, and setteth his heart

upon it: lest he cry against thee unto the LORD, and it be sin unto thee. (Deuteronomy 24:14–15)

Woe unto him that buildeth his house by unrighteousness, and his chambers by wrong; that useth his neighbour's service without wages, and giveth him not for his work. (Jeremiah 22:13)

The employee also has obligations toward his or her employer. We should give the boss an honest day's labor for the pay we are to receive. We expect the employer to be fair with us, but we also should be fair with him or her. It is akin to theft for the employee to waste time while on the clock when the employer is paying his or her wages. He or she may be whiling away the day on personal phone calls or surfing the Internet for personal interests. If he or she is consuming social media for personal pleasure or idly chatting with other employees, that person is depriving the company of productivity. While the employer is paying our wages, we owe it to him or her and to the company to do our best to fulfill our duties. We should give the best performance we are capable of in exchange for the wages agreed upon.

We should not accept a job on the basis of a promised wage, but then gossip and criticize the boss for not paying us more. We agreed upon that wage. To criticize the wage is to also criticize oneself. It is similar to married people who criticize their spouses. They chose that person for marriage; thus they are criticizing not only the spouse, but also their own judgment.

Consider the story Jesus told about the hired workers. Some hired out in the morning for the wage of one penny for the day; others were hired later for the same wage. (See Matthew

20:1–16.) When the day was done and payment was given out, the ones who hired out early complained about receiving only a penny when the other workers, who had worked fewer hours, also received a penny. They had no basis for complaint. They had received the agreed upon wage.

Ethical conduct requires fairness from both the employer and the employee. We should do what is right, for that is the ethical thing to do. And Christians should be known as individuals who always endeavor to do what is right.

CHAPTER TWELVE

ETHICS OF STEWARDSHIP— TIME, FINANCES, AND TALENTS

> Let a man so account of us, as of the ministers of Christ, and stewards of the mysteries of God. Moreover it is required in stewards, that a man be found faithful. (I Corinthians 4:1–2)

Being responsible with one's time, finances, and talents is a significant aspect of Christian ethics. A Christian cannot be sloppy in these and still be ethical in his or her conduct.

People observe our behaviors in these areas of life and they make conclusions about us based on how we handle such responsibilities. Their conclusions ultimately establish our reputation—whether honestly deserved or mischaracterized. However, our faithfulness in these areas of responsibility is the result of our character. Our ethics as they pertain to how we handle our money, time, and talents should demonstrate an exceptional inner strength of sterling character.

Paul's observation about stewards is classic: if they desire to be a steward, they must be faithful. They should be faithful in their character, which affects their conduct and habits. Stewardship, then, involves one's faithfulness in all these aspects of life because faithfulness and stewardship are inseparably connected.

FAITHFUL IN THE STEWARDSHIP OF TIME

Time is something every person has in common; nobody has more or less time than anyone else. Everyone has the same number of hours every week—168 hours. We have the opportunity as individuals to decide exactly how we will spend those 168 hours. If we choose to waste some of them, that is our choice. If we choose to spend our time on hobbies, that also is our choice. By our own sense of priorities we also determine the number of hours we allocate to Jesus Christ and His church. Time is an invaluable commodity, so we should carefully consider how we spend it. Are we faithful in our stewardship of time spent?

Let us briefly consider the ethics associated with various ways in which a person might spend his or her time.

Responsibility to Spend Time with God

First, a Christian should be faithful in his responsibility of spending time with the Lord.

A person could examine his or her stewardship of time on the basis of the principle of the tithe, which is "a tenth." Without trying to force our time into a legalistic formula, it seems like a reasonable starting point for evaluating how one spends his or her time. In such an analysis, consider spending an hour of prayer every day, five hours a week of church attendance, and half an hour of daily Bible reading. That would put a person near the 10 percent mark of 168 hours. Add to that time spent witnessing, volunteering for the church, and other godly endeavors and it would definitely place one above the 10 percent mark.

Is the concept of tithing our time really biblical though? Did not the Lord place us in this world to be salt and light? It seems quite compartmentalized to separate the time we spend into a spiritual part and a secular part. It seems as if believers ought to spend most of their time influencing the secular with the spiritual. How could we truly track that?

Perhaps it is not appropriate to track our time from a legalistic perspective. Instead, we should consider it important to be faithful stewards of all the time God has given us. We certainly need "down time" for relaxation daily, but we should avoid the temptation to become lethargic and slothful. We should generously spend our time on behalf of Jesus Christ and the work of His church.

Spending time in personal prayer is our foremost responsibility as believers. Prayer is our lifeline of connection to God. It is through prayer our spiritual growth in Christ and development as a Christian take root. Without prayer, the time spent for other endeavors on behalf of the church becomes superficial and lacks significance. Prayer gives meaning and spiritual strength and energy to every dimension of our lives as Christian believers.

Consider the time we give to corporate church attendance, worship, and fellowship with the body of Christ. The Scriptures urge us to be faithful in our assembling together

(Hebrews 10:25). Corporate activities with the body of Christ are important both to the health of the local congregation and also to the health of the individuals. We need the experience of praying and worshiping together, and we also need the growth experienced through corporate fellowship with other believers. Christian ethics requires faithful cooperation and participation within a local assembly of believers. No person is an island; each one is a part of the whole community and vitally connected.

In Paul's first epistle to the Corinthians, he wrote with the assumption that the believers would regularly congregate together. (See I Corinthians 11:18, 20, 33–34; 14:26.) Regular worship services with the local assembly members gathered together is a vital aspect of the Christian experience. The quality time we spend with the local church is a blessing to us and to our fellow believers, and it fulfills a responsibility.

Responsibility to Spend Time with and for Others

> As every man hath received the gift, even so
> minister the same one to another, as good stewards
> of the manifold grace of God. (I Peter 4:10)

Our responsibilities to the local church are not limited only to our responsibility to faithfully worship Jesus Christ. We also have a responsibility to minister to our brothers and sisters in Christ. God has given every individual in the body of Christ gifts as He has determined (I Corinthians 12:1–7). When God gives a gift to an individual, God has the edification of the entire body of Christ in view. Consider I Corinthians 12:7 in the

English Standard Version: "To each is given the manifestation of the Spirit for the common good."

When we gather together for worship and fellowship, we never know what needs may exist within our fellow believers. They may be in desperate need of encouragement. We might be able to speak a word of encouragement to someone who needs it even though we may not be aware of the need. That is how the body of Christ is designed to work—each member supplying what he or she can, which ministers to the entire body (I Corinthians 14:12, 26; I Peter 4:10–11).

> From whom the whole body fitly joined together and compacted by that which every joint supplieth, according to the effectual working in the measure of every part, maketh increase of the body unto the edifying of itself in love. (Ephesians 4:16)

As faithful stewards of Jesus Christ, we have an ethical obligation to the Lord and also to the local church. We should resist the temptation to squander our time selfishly upon ourselves. Rather, we should spend it generously and selflessly on behalf of the Lord and His body. And yet, we have another ethical obligation regarding the time we spend in life: a responsibility to ourselves.

Responsibility to Spend Time for Ourselves

In Mark 6:31, Jesus said, "Come ye yourselves apart into a desert place, and rest a while: for there were many coming and going, and they had no leisure so much as to eat." We have an obligation to ourselves to set aside time for rest and spiritual recharging. The Lord who made our human bodies knows our need for physical rest and relaxation.

> Regarding Mark 6:31, Vance Havner once observed, "If we don't come apart; we will come apart." (www. christianquotes.info/quotes-by-author/vance-havner-quotes, accessed June 21, 2016)

Some individuals feel guilty about taking time off for rest and relaxation, but our bodies need rest. God established the entire concept of the Sabbath at Creation not because He was weary, but because He understood the frail nature of the human frame. (See Genesis 2:1–3.) Humankind was not made to work seven days a week without rest.

It is interesting that in recent years proponents of various weight-loss diets have recognized and promoted the necessity of getting plenty of rest every night. They have come to believe getting sufficient rest every night aids the human body in managing weight, especially in weight loss.

We have a responsibility to ourselves to provide sufficient opportunities to get the rest our bodies need. Many people—including Christians—are workaholics and almost disdain the idea of sleep and taking time off. However, if we are to be healthy and productive long-term, we must ensure we provide adequate time for our bodies to rest. We should strive to faithfully plan for and set aside time for

- a good night of sleep daily;
- regular times of rest or recreation sometime through the day or evening;

- regular opportunities to get away from the stress and wearisome pace of life through vacations or brief escapes from life's routines.

FAITHFUL IN FINANCIAL STEWARDSHIP

Christians also have an ethical obligation to be faithful in their financial stewardship. As it is with the time believers expend in life, they also have obligations regarding how they spend their money. We have financial responsibilities toward God, toward others, and toward ourselves.

Responsibility to God with How We Handle Our Finances

> Will a man rob God? Yet ye have robbed me. But ye say, Wherein have we robbed thee? In tithes and offerings. (Malachi 3:8)

Does the idea of robbing God seem strange? Admittedly, it is difficult to perceive the ability of a person to rob the Sovereign of the universe, but it is indeed possible. Malachi told the people they had robbed God by withholding tithes and offerings.

The tithe belongs to the Lord (Leviticus 27:30). It is not an amount of our money that we set aside to give to God. Rather, it is an amount of the Lord's money that belongs to Him. He is waiting to see whether we will do what is ethically right by returning it to Him for His work on earth. We have not even given of our finances to God until we exceed the first tenth of our income, for that amount already belongs to Him.

Our first responsibility with regard to financial stewardship involves returning the tithe to the Lord. Our second financial responsibility is to set aside an offering for the work of God. It is ethical for a Christian to be faithful in how he handles these finances.

It is certainly true that not every Christian has the same ability to give. Some individuals are blessed with more monetary resources with which they can bless the work of God. Others have only meager amounts above their tithing that they are able to give to the church. One thing is always consistent, however: God blesses the cheerful giver. He blesses the giver not on the basis of the amount he or she gives but according to the attitude and spirit with which the person gives it. (See II Corinthians 9:7.) Someone has said God looks less at the amounts we give than He does to the amount we have left over after giving. That was the case with the widow who gave a pittance—the widow's mite. Jesus praised her as having given more than them all.

We also know Jesus said we will receive according to the same measure we give (Luke 6:38). If we give stingily, we will only receive stingily, but if we generously give we shall receive generously.

> Give, and it shall be given unto you; good measure, pressed down, and shaken together, and running over, shall men give into your bosom. For with the same measure that ye mete withal it shall be measured to you again. (Luke 6:38)

Responsibility toward Others with How We Handle Our Finances

Because we all comprise the body of Jesus Christ on earth, the church, when one member of the body hurts, we all hurt. When one member is joyful, we all share in that joy. We all are one body. Consequently, when one member is in financial need, the other members of the body come to the assistance of the one in need. That is how the human body works, each organ working for the good of the entire body, and that is how the church works.

Our financial obligations are not to ourselves alone, nor do they exist only of paying our tithes and giving in a few offerings. We have an obligation to help our brothers and sisters when they are in need. John wrote, "But if anyone has the world's goods and sees his brother in need, yet closes his heart against him, how does God's love abide in him?" (I John 3:17, ESV). People will know we are Christians by our demonstrated love one for another (John 13:35). If we love our fellow believers, we will not abandon them in their hour of financial crisis.

Since the church is the body of Christ and since we are to faithfully meet together for worship and fellowship, we all have a financial obligation to the church. There are associated financial expenses with having a church, and we all should participate in paying them. Someone has to pay the church mortgage, the electricity bill, the water bill, the insurance bill, and others. These expenses were incurred on behalf of the entire church assembly; we cannot assume someone else will pay the bills. We have a responsibility toward our fellow believers to assist with the financial obligations of the church.

Also, there are costs involved in operating church services to which sinners can come, feel conviction, and respond to the drawing Spirit of the Lord. We have an obligation to help reach the lost. Part of that obligation involves giving to help pay the bills, purchase tracts and literature, and conduct outreach programs. It is not only the "preacher's job" to save the lost; we all share in that responsibility.

We must not neglect the material needs of the local church. There also are financial needs that extend beyond the local congregation. There are missionary endeavors to fund and special ministries we should assist.

The local church is not a place for us to show up on occasion when convenient, enjoy the service, and scoot out the back door. We have an obligation to do our part financially as a member of that local assembly. We also need to pray for the church leaders, be faithful to attend, assist with needs around the facilities, and support the leaders spiritually and emotionally.

Responsibility to Ourselves with How We Handle Our Finances

We also have an obligation to ourselves regarding how we handle our finances. Our first obligation should be to return to God the tithe, which belongs to Him. Second, we should always plan to give in offerings above and beyond that amount and be prepared to participate in special offerings. However, good and faithful stewardship also requires we set aside an amount for our own future savings.

A person should only incur the expenses he or she is able to pay in a timely fashion. Sometimes it is inevitable that we incur unexpected expenses, but it is debilitating to load oneself with excessive debt. It stresses the cash flow so severely one is hard pressed to meet all his or her financial obligations. It is stressful to live so strapped financially. However, if a person has exercised good stewardship and set aside savings for emergencies or financially difficult seasons, the stress will be diminished greatly.

Good financial stewardship begins with having a personal budget and understanding one's personal expenses. Next, he or she should pay tithes and give offerings, have a plan for paying other monthly expenses, and set aside some savings. It is unethical for a person to be a spendthrift and then expect others to care for them when their sources of revenue dry up.

FAITHFUL IN TALENTS

Finally, a Christian should exercise faithful stewardship to use the gifts with which God has endowed him or her—talents. No one is indispensable, but God has a plan for every person in the body of Christ. Some are gifted administrators and some are great teachers and preachers. Some are gifted musically to sing or play instruments. Some are blessed with artistic and creative gifts. Some are great with technology applications for the work of the church. God gives many gifts to His people to bless the overall work of His church.

God gives spiritual gifts (I Corinthians 12; Romans 12), gifts of administration, helps, and governments (I Corinthians 12), and gifts of ministries (Ephesians 4:7–12). All these gifts He gives "severally as he will" (I Corinthians 12:11). It is His decision. He knows what His church needs and He provides gifts liberally for the spiritual growth and edification of His body (Ephesians 4:12).

There is something for everyone to do in the body of Christ. All are important members of His church. Some individuals feel useless; they feel they are without talent, but that is never the case. Perhaps they have not discovered their talents, but

God gives gifts to every member of the body. We all have a vital place and role to fill.

What our talents may be is not important. It is important we dedicate them diligently to the work of the Lord. It is important we are good stewards of the gifts with which God has entrusted us.

STEWARDS OF OUR CHARACTER AND REPUTATION

Good stewards will be faithful in all matters of time, finance, and talents. As they demonstrate faithfulness in all these areas, they will demonstrate the purity of their character. As others observe the faithfulness of Christians, they will form opinions of their character, which contributes to the Christians' reputation. We cannot directly control the reputation others assign to us, but we can do everything within our power to live with pure character and faithfulness to God and to others.

Why should we care what others think of us, especially since we cannot directly control it? We do everything within our power to safeguard our reputation because it is a reflection upon the reputation of Christ and His church.

There are many areas that can trip up believers in our contemporary culture. We should always be on guard to protect ourselves from these temptations and the attack of the enemy.

One of the dangerous areas of involvement in our day stems from social media, such as Facebook, Twitter, and others. These avenues of social media contain numerous potential pitfalls.

First, social media are time consumers. What a waste of time they can be! It is certainly not wrong to spend time with social media, and there can be good things that come from it.

Still, we must guard the excessive use of social media so we do not become victims of its wasteful time consumption.

Second, some people on social media have impure motives. They are out to entice individuals into areas of immoral or questionable conduct. They speak of inappropriate activities and post immodest pictures. We need to avoid these individuals.

Third, "friendships" are formed on social media, and some of those could potentially become detrimental to marital relationships. At best, they sometimes create distrust and jealousy; at worst, they may entice married individuals into inappropriate relationships.

We must carefully guard our reputation and take precautions against exposing ourselves to temptation. There are enough sources of temptation in this world without our opening the door to additional ones.

We should do all within our power to operate in every area of life with only the highest measures of ethical conduct. After all, the greatest desire of a Christian is that at the judgment he or she will hear the immortal words, "Well done, thou good and faithful servant . . . enter thou into the joy of thy lord" (Matthew 25:21).

CHAPTER THIRTEEN

MAINTAINING ONE'S MENTAL, PHYSICAL, AND SPIRITUAL WELL-BEING IN CHRIST

I beseech you therefore, brethren, by the mercies of God, that ye present your bodies a living sacrifice, holy, acceptable unto God, which is your reasonable service. And be not conformed to this world: but be ye transformed by the renewing of your mind, that ye may prove what is that good, and acceptable, and perfect, will of God. (Romans 12:1–2)

In this study of Christian principles of conduct we should consider some ethical obligations every person owes himself or herself. People are capable of treating others with proper decorum and respect only when they first respect themselves. Insecure people with low self-esteem will invariably reflect their lack of personal confidence in how they treat others.

It is important Christians have a proper self-respect that motivates them to give themselves without reservation to the service of God. Paul called offering our bodies as a living sacrifice our "reasonable service." It is unreasonable for Christians to give anything less than their best to God. Christ gave His all for us. We should discipline ourselves to be able to give our best to God mentally, physically, and spiritually.

MENTALLY ALERT

> Wherefore gird up the loins of your mind.
> (I Peter 1:13)

First, we are to discipline our mind. Peter wrote that we should "gird up the loins" of our mind. How vital it is that we control the thoughts we allow ourselves to dwell upon! We will become exactly the kind of person we are in the realm of our thinking (Proverbs 23:7). The discipline (or lack thereof) we enact in the mind is apparent in our personal and public conduct.

The translation of I Peter 1:13 in the New International Version is interesting: "Therefore, prepare your minds for action; be self-controlled; set your hope fully on the grace to be given you when Jesus Christ is revealed."

So how do we prepare our mind for action?

First, we discipline our mind to dwell on good, wholesome, positive thoughts. In his epistle to the church at Philippi, Paul wrote: "Finally, brethren, whatsoever things are true, whatsoever things are honest, whatsoever things are just, whatsoever things are pure, whatsoever things are lovely, whatsoever things are of good report; if there be any virtue, and if there be any praise, think on these things" (Philippians 4:8). We should think on

1. things that are *true,*
2. things that are *honest,*
3. things that are *just,*
4. things that are *pure,*
5. things that are *lovely,*
6. things that are of *good report,*
7. things that are *virtuous, and*
8. things that are *praiseworthy.*

How pleasant to limit our thoughts to only those things that edify! If we will choose to dwell on these eight positive themes, we will harness the potential and direction of our mind.

Second, we discipline our mind to learn the Scriptures. "Study to shew thyself approved unto God, a workman that needeth not to be ashamed, rightly dividing the word of truth" (II Timothy 2:15). Jesus said, "Search the scriptures; for in them ye think ye have eternal life: and they are they which testify of me" (John 5:39).

Learning the Scriptures is the surest way to internalize the life-changing principles of the Bible. For a Christian to live a shameless life and enjoy the approval of God, he must strive to learn and live by the Word of God. The Bible is to the Christian what a roadmap is to a traveler, what law journals are to a lawyer, and what medical journals are to a doctor. The Bible is essential to give us vital direction and instruction for the Christian life.

Third, our mind is transformed by the Holy Spirit. "And be not conformed to this world: but be ye transformed by the renewing of your mind, that ye may prove what is that good, and acceptable, and perfect, will of God" (Romans 12:2).

After coming to a saving knowledge of and relationship with Jesus Christ, our mind is not the same. When we receive the Holy Ghost we experience a dramatic mental transformation. Our thoughts are monitored and influenced by the resident Spirit of Christ. Rather than dwelling continually on the typical thoughts of the carnal life, we begin to think from a spiritual perspective. The things we once craved in our carnality we no longer desire, and we begin to hunger for the spiritual things of life. The spiritual once held no attraction for us, but our taste and hunger change.

Fourth, we love God with all our mind. "And he answering said, Thou shalt love the Lord thy God with all thy heart, and with all thy soul, and with all thy strength, and with all thy mind; and thy neighbour as thyself" (Luke 10:27). (See also Matthew 22:37; Mark 12:30.)

Love is one of the foremost characteristics of God, and it is an integral part of our new redeemed nature. God *is* love (I John 4:8, 16). Because we receive the Spirit of God into our heart, we also receive His nature to love.

We love fellow Christians with a profound sense of affection. We also love the lost and love our enemies, for the love of Christ is in our heart. In addition to these new and fresh dimensions of love, we love God intensely. We love God with all our heart, soul, strength, and mind. Because of our love for Jesus Christ, we desire to live ethically toward Him, as well as toward all people.

In addition to the above four ways we prepare our mind for action, we have to be vigilant and avoid Satan's deceptive traps. We must protect our mind from the pollutions of this world.

David Jeremiah wrote an article titled "The Porno Plague." In his article, Jeremiah gave four suggestions to help a person to remain pure though surrounded by the impurities of a world filled with pornography: (1) covenant with your eyes; (2) consecrate your mind; (3) commit yourself to Bible memorization; (4) counteract Satan's strategy in your life. He correctly observed, "The mind is the battleground upon which every moral and spiritual battle is fought. Our thinking ultimately determines our character" (*The Rebirth of America*, The Arthur S. DeMoss Foundation).

These definite actions and steps will enable us to achieve mental alertness. Peter essentially referred to the subject of mental alertness when he cautioned about the tactics of Satan in his first epistle: "Be sober, be vigilant; because your adversary the devil, as a roaring lion, walketh about, seeking whom he may devour" (I Peter 5:8). We can achieve a sober awareness and vigilance only by disciplining our mind to follow godly principles and to reject the allurements of temptation.

PHYSICALLY FIT

We also are responsible for our physical fitness. Although a person's level of physical fitness often is not equated with his mental and spiritual needs, weak physical stamina hinders us mentally and spiritually. It is important we do our best to care for our physical needs.

Paul stated that the exercise of the body profits little, but it is profitable.

> For bodily exercise profiteth little: but godliness
> is profitable unto all things, having promise of
> the life that now is, and of that which is to come.
> (I Timothy 4:8)

Considering the typical Middle Eastern diet, it is a safe assumption Paul did not experience the problem North Americans have with high-fat content in their Western diet. Primarily because of the inordinate amount of fat and calories in the typical Western diet, Americans struggle with obesity like few other people of the earth.

There are numerous reasons why Christians should exercise self-control and discipline, and should avoid obesity and poor physical habits:

1. We may live longer and have more opportunity to work for Christ if we care properly for our physical body.
2. We will generally feel better and have more energy to live and work for Christ if we are in good physical condition.
3. We will reflect a more positive self-image, and we will represent Christ and His church in a better and more positive light.
4. It is better for us that we keep our body in good physical condition. We will enjoy our life more.

Regular exercise and following a healthy, wholesome diet will enhance the mental and spiritual aspects of our life as well as the physical.

SPIRITUALLY SOUND

The *American Heritage Dictionary* defines the word *sound* as follows: "Free from defect, decay, or damage; in good condition. Free from disease or injury. Having a firm basis; unshakable." It goes on to define the word further as "Thorough; complete. Free from moral defect; upright. Worthy of confidence; trustworthy."

As Christians we need to be sound, solid, and unshakable in our spiritual life. The only way we can experience such a state is by building our lives upon the only sure foundation—Jesus Christ and His Word. There is nothing else that can assure us of integrity or wholeness in our lives. But when we build our lives upon Him, we are secure.

These disciplines will empower us to have the right mental attitudes toward ourselves, which also will assist us in treating others ethically. We should discipline our mind, body, and spirit to be the best they can be. Only then will we be in the best frame of mind to treat others with the love, kindness, and respect they deserve.

CHAPTER FOURTEEN

ETHICS IN MINISTRY

This chapter is not intended to substitute for the previous thirteen; neither is it meant to stand alone. In this chapter we will consider specific applications of the principles covered previously as they apply to ministry. We also will point out additional ethical obligations ministers of the gospel assume. It is vital to understand the principles previously covered in order to accurately and appropriately apply them to a minister's ethical obligations.

The ministry is a high calling from God, not from men or human institutions. Speaking of his apostleship, Paul wrote to the Galatians, "Paul, an apostle, (not of men, neither by man, but by Jesus Christ, and God the Father, who raised him from the dead;)" (Galatians 1:1). The ministry is not a mere choice of vocation or job; it involves the call of God upon a person's life.

Biblically, perhaps the most evident passage referencing "the call" is the Apostle Paul's Damascus Road experience. In Acts 9, we read. . . . "Saul is my chosen instrument" (Acts 9:15). . . . That is "the call"—a unique, divine assignment given by God for his purposes. (Natasha Sistrunk Robinson, "Answering the Call of God," www.christianitytoday. com, accessed June 23, 2016)

Ministry is a call from God that carries important duties and obligations. Fulfilling these responsibilities—and how one goes about fulfilling them—comprises the core of ministerial ethics. Although they flow out of the stream of the larger topic of Christian ethics and involve primarily the same principles, let us explore some of their finer details. To do so, we will examine them on four different levels: minister to the community; minister to the layperson; minister to minister; and minister to organizational leadership.

Minister's Ethics toward the Community

The minister of the gospel has a responsibility to the community in which he or she lives and ministers. Even if the minister is not a pastor, unchurched individuals will judge the local church, the organization, and even Christians in general by the minister's behavior. The minister's persona and conduct can be a blessing for or a curse against the evangelistic work of the local church in the community.

The minister should pay his bills and meet all his financial obligations. He should be timely, diligent, and cheerful in the handling of his financial transactions in the community. The local stores should recognize him or her as a conscientious person who is reliable to keep his or her commitments, whether financial obligations or other commitments. Never should they have the opportunity to view a minister as a scoundrel or a cheat. They should see the minister as dependable and one who pays his or her bills—and that, on time. To do otherwise is damaging to the work of the church and the reputation of the body of the Lord Jesus Christ.

I knew a man who took a church pastorate, which included a terrible building full of trash. When he went to the power company to have the electricity turned on for the building, they refused. They indicated the previous pastor had promised to fix certain things about the building when they turned the power on the last time. Unfortunately, the work was never done according to the company. In a polite conversation, the power company official finally agreed to run power to a single utility pole for the purpose of running power tools. The previous pastor had left a bad impression on them, but the new pastor was able to begin mending the relationship.

The minister's attitude and disposition should be among the most cheerful, pleasant, and attractive in the community. People in the local community should be glad to see the minister coming. Never should they dread it, knowing he or she will be sour, unpleasant, and gossiping or complaining about something. All people enjoy being around others who make them feel good. When the minister leaves the business, hospital, or home, the people whom he or she has encountered should be edified and blessed that the minister was there.

The minister of the gospel should continually be aware of his or her status as an ambassador of Jesus Christ (II Corinthians 5:20). We are His representatives in this world. People will learn about Him through what they see and experience in us;

they will judge Him based on how well we represent Him and His cause. We should represent Him well and conscientiously work as His hands and feet in a hurting world that desperately needs to hear the gospel.

Minister's Ethics toward the Layperson

What are the ethical responsibilities of the minister toward the layperson? The layperson could be a member of the church the minister pastors, or he or she could be one who attends another church. If the minister is not a pastor, it could be someone who attends church with the minister or someone who attends another church. How is the minister to treat others who are not ministers?

First, the minister never has cause to be aloof from or arrogant toward the laity. That Christ has called a minister into pulpit ministry does not make the minister an elite prima donna. Both the minister and the layperson are equal members of the body of Jesus Christ; both have the calling of God upon their lives. They only have different callings and different functions within the body. But no member of the body has a right or a reason to disparage the other members of the body. All are important. All are loved by Christ and have their role and place within the function of the entire body. (See I Corinthians 12.)

> For the body is not one member, but many. If the foot shall say, Because I am not the hand, I am not of the body; is it therefore not of the body? And if the ear shall say, Because I am not the eye, I am not of the body; is it therefore not of the body? If the whole body were an eye, where were the

hearing? If the whole were hearing, where were the smelling? But now hath God set the members every one of them in the body, as it hath pleased him. (I Corinthians 12:14–18)

Arrogance displeases the Lord. He hates the proud look (Proverbs 6:16–17). (See also Job 40:12; Psalm 101:5; Proverbs 21:4.) Sometimes ministers are insecure and uncertain of themselves and they unintentionally cause others to perceive them as proud or arrogant. They have no cause to be insecure. The Lord has called them into a special work of ministry within the body of Christ. God knew they were capable of fulfilling the calling on their lives, otherwise He would not have called them. Ministers should be confident and secure, knowing the Lord has faith and confidence in them to perform His calling and work.

Part of the calling God gives all of us is to love everybody. Why would we want to give some individuals the sense we do not care about them or their needs? Let the ministers be friendly and loving, showing Christ's love to the world—especially to their brothers and sisters in Christ.

Second, ministers should inspire confidence and blessing in the lives of the laypersons with whom they come in contact. Ministers should inspire fellow believers with the same sense of joy, love, and kindness with which they inspire people of the community.

"But should I be friendly toward the members of another apostolic congregation?" Absolutely! Why would we want to ignore, disrespect, or avoid other members of the body of Christ? One could say, "Yes, but they might interpret my friendliness as an invitation to leave their church to come to the one I pastor." Obviously, we cannot control how people interpret our kindness and friendliness. They probably will interpret our friendliness as an invitation to visit only if they already are looking for an excuse or reason to leave the church they attend. But that is no excuse for us to be snobbish or aloof from them. Clearly, if they were to show up at your church, you would have an obligation to make clear to them they must return and discuss their concerns with their pastor, which is not you. Further, that other pastor deserves a call from you so he or she does not have reason to distrust your motives.

It is repeated often in this book, but treat them and the other pastor as you want to be treated. There is no reason to be unkind. Unkindness does not reflect the proper attitude and position of a Christian. Even when explaining to an errant member of another congregation the need to return to his or her church and pastor, it can be done with kindness and a Christlike spirit. If the person returns to his or her pastor and both the person and the pastor agree they need to make a change, only then should you welcome them back.

If members from another church persist in coming even though they know they do not have your blessing or that of their pastor, you must handle the situation properly. You and their pastor should come to an amenable approach to try to salvage their souls, not destroy them. Why would either pastor—who are both in the soul-saving business—want to destroy an individual over human differences, even if those differences are rooted in rebellion? Work together to find an approach for helping them. Jesus Christ loves them and died for their sins as He did for the sins of the whole world. We should love even those who are unlovable, for that is what Christ has called us to do. If we limit our outreach to only those who deserve love and salvation, there will be none left to love or save, including ourselves.

In the instance a layperson insists there is a moral problem with the other pastor or that he or she is no longer preaching truth, the situation must be handled carefully. The principle to follow is found in I Timothy 5:19: "Against an elder receive not an accusation, but before two or three witnesses."

You must not accept the person's accusations without additional corroboration. It does not matter how nice they are, how attractive they appear, or how financially secure they seem to be. Ethics require that you first follow the Scriptures. You have no idea what is actually happening in the other church. Only if there are two or more witnesses should you even accept their accusation.

If there are not "two or three witnesses," follow the previous steps of trying to salvage the wandering person's soul. Trust the other pastor and work with him or her toward that objective. If the other charges are true, they will come out in time. It is not your place to serve as chief investigator. Trust your brother or sister and work with him or her the best you can.

If an accusatory report does come with the required "two or three witnesses," turn the matter over to your district authorities. Trust them to proceed by following the best course of action. As for you, continue to trust your fellow minister and pray for him or her. Follow your usual course of ethical practices. Call the pastor and work with him or her to determine how to address the problem with the wayward believers. Do not raise their accusations with the pastor. Leave that to district leadership and try not to become involved in a potentially explosive situation.

Minister's Ethics toward Fellow Ministers

Ethical conduct between fellow ministers of the gospel can be a difficult and sensitive topic, but it does not need to be. The same principles we apply to other topics of ethical conduct apply here. We should love others and treat them as we would like to be—and often expect to be—treated.

Consider this: contemplate the people to whom you minister whether as pastor, evangelist, or teacher. What kind of conduct do you expect from them? Do you expect them to be loving and kind toward others? Do you expect them to be respectful toward all people, and especially toward you and all the ministry? Do you expect them to be good stewards of their time and finances as well as generous givers into the work of the kingdom of God? Your expectations of their attitudes and conduct are reflections of the attitudes and conduct you should exemplify toward your fellow ministers—and indeed, toward all people.

You might object, "But that minister doesn't share all the same convictions I have." "She believes differently than I about several biblical doctrines." "He is not friendly." "She never attends meetings at my church." Really? Their differences or possible failings in attitude or conduct excuse your attitude and conduct? Is that what the Bible teaches?

> We who are strong have an obligation to bear with the failings of the weak, and not to please ourselves. Let each of us please his neighbor for his good, to build him up. . . . May the God of endurance and encouragement grant you to live in such harmony with one another, in accord with Christ Jesus. (Romans 15:1–5, ESV)

Many individuals have read Ezekiel 3:9 and similar verses and observed what God said about His prophet's head being "harder than flint." There seems to be a possible correlation between that verse and the fact many ministers seem to generally be hardheaded and stubborn. Notice the entry regarding Ezekiel 3:9 in *The Bible Knowledge Commentary*:

> God also said He would make Ezekiel's forehead like the hardest stone, harder than flint. Figuratively "forehead" expresses determination or defiance. . . . Ezekiel's determination would not waver when beset by opposition. "Flint," the hardest stone in Palestine, was used by Israel for knives (cf. Josh. 5:2–3) and other implements. Ezekiel's God-given strength and determination would withstand any opposition (cf. Jer. 1:18). (Charles H. Dyer, "Ezekiel," in *The Bible Knowledge Commentary: An Exposition of the Scriptures*, eds. J. F. Walvoord and R. B. Zuck, vol. 1 [Wheaton, IL: Victor Books, 1985], 1231–1232)

One can hardly argue against the idea God generally calls individuals into ministry who possess strong determination and strength of will and purpose to perform God's call. However, just because a preacher might be somewhat hardheaded does not excuse belligerence, especially toward his or her fellow ministers of the gospel. Sometimes we just have to agree to disagree. We do not have to be disagreeable in our disagreements with others.

How should ministers interact with one another? They should always interact with the love of God, kindness, compassion, concern, and respect—just to name several characteristics. These are qualities every Christian should possess and demonstrate toward their fellow Christians. Why would we not expect ministers to conduct themselves with the same attitudes and characteristics?

It would be difficult to narrow these qualities to the most vital, most important ones. If I were to try to narrow them to a couple of the most important, it would have to be "love" and "kindness." I would choose love and kindness because these two qualities prompt and motivate an individual also to exhibit the others.

Respect is also important. But one suggests, "He does not deserve respect." Is that how the Lord Jesus treated us? We all have received much from the Lord we did not deserve. In fact, the only thing we deserve is eternal judgment, but Jesus loved us and worked with us nevertheless. Try this: if you cannot give the minister the full respect you afford to others, could you at least give him or her the minimum measure of respect? Could you give that person the respect afforded to all who are created in the image of God? We all are His creation, and as someone observed, "God don't make no junk!" You never can tell; your appreciation for the person might even grow over time.

We do not have to be best friends with every minister we know. But we should love them as Christ loves them and tolerate whatever differences may exist between us. We should respect them as ones created in the image of God, and pray for them as brothers or sisters in Christ. Is that too much to ask? Jesus didn't think so.

When Judas came to betray Jesus, Christ knew exactly what his intentions were, but He still addressed Judas as "friend." (See Matthew 26:48–50.) Such an extreme example, yet Jesus called Judas His friend! Surely no person has treated us as badly as Judas treated Jesus. Can we at least extend to every person a modicum of respect and courtesy? After all, they are our brothers and sisters and co-laborers in ministry.

Although certainly not intended to be an exhaustive list, here are several principles of ethical conduct, which should guide interactions between ministers:

- *Trust.* Ministers should live in a way to build their trustworthiness, and they should readily exercise trust toward their fellow ministers. They should be quick to trust, slow to distrust. They should be slow to believe negative reports about their colleagues in ministry. There are times when negative reports will prove to be true and may require action on a minister's part. However, when one hears a gossipy, slanderous report, it is time to give the involved brother or sister the benefit of any doubt. A minister should reject the report and support his or her brother or sister in Christ. Further, it is inappropriate to spread the negative rumor. Even if it proves to be true, we need to demonstrate love, have compassion, and pray for those affected and those who are suffering because of the situation.
- *Communication.* Ministers within a particular city, area, or region should keep the communication lines open between one another. It is never healthy to withdraw from communication or fellowship. Interaction enables ministers to maintain trust and appreciation for one another. It enables them to know of mutual concerns that affect all the ministry, and opens up a needed dimension of inclusive ministerial fellowship. If the communication

lines are kept open, one pastor is quicker to contact another pastor should an ethical concern arise out of the actions of laypersons. When needed contact is not made—for instance, when a member from one church shows up unexpectedly at another church—it cultivates distrust and engenders suspicions about one's motives.

- *Respect.* Ministers should respect one another, including some with whom differences may exist. Every minister has differing gifts, talents, backgrounds, and interests. It is OK to be different; we are not all the same. We must learn to respect and trust one another and grant liberties to believe and act differently on non-essential matters. Perhaps some conflicts arise out of differences of where ones may draw the line of "essential" versus "non-essential." However, unless it is a violation of the fundamental plan of salvation or other clearly stated biblical absolutes, we need to grant liberty as far as is conscientiously possible.

- *Love.* Ministers should love one another—even those with whom they may not agree on every point. You do not have to agree with another person to love that individual. After all, Jesus Christ loved us while we were yet sinners and unlovable. (See Romans 5:8.) "Beloved, if God so loved us, we ought also to love one another. . . . If we love one another, God dwelleth in us, and his love is perfected in us" (I John 4:11–12).

- *Cooperation.* Ministers should always strive to maintain a spirit of cooperation with fellow ministers. All should bear in mind we are all on the same team working for the same cause. We should celebrate with our fellow ministers in their successes and weep with them in their losses. Never should we allow jealousy to arise within our spirits causing us to resent any good things being experienced by a neighboring church. Rejoice together!

In 1964, the general conference of the United Pentecostal Church International adopted a position paper containing a code of ethics for ministers. The intent of the paper was to provide principles to guide a minister, not laws to govern them. Drawing from that position paper, we discover the following points of principle to assist in guiding the conduct of ministers among one another. Ministers should always

- endeavor to be a good minister of the Lord Jesus Christ;
- prepare themselves in body, mind, and spirit;
- safeguard the good name of the ministry;
- speak the truth in love;
- live honestly and avoid embarrassing debts;
- keep as sacred all confidences shared with them;
- exercise the authority of a spiritual leader rather than that of a dictator;
- seek to minister rather than to be ministered unto;
- place service above salary and personal recognition;
- place the unity and welfare of the church above their own personal welfare;
- seek to lead the church to accept its full responsibility for community and world service;
- seek to build the church without discrediting other churches;
- refrain from soliciting members from other churches;
- refrain from casting reflection on other ministers;

- refrain from unethical competition with another minister over a call to a pastorate;
- sever pastoral relations with former parishioners following their resignation;
- refrain from making pastoral contacts in the field of another pastor without his or her knowledge and consent;
- refrain from accepting the pastorate of a United Pentecostal Church unless it is in accord with the Articles of Faith and Constitution of the general church body;
- refrain from using their influence to alienate the church or any portion of the church constituents from fellowshipping or supporting the United Pentecostal Church International;
- honorably withdraw from UPCI ministerial membership and association with the local UPCI church assembly if their convictions change and are in conflict with the teachings of the UPCI.

Simply stated, ministers should love, trust, and respect their ministerial colleagues. If one is going to be in contact with a member from another church, it should be only with the highest of ethical intentions and conduct. He should contact the person's pastor and make every effort to work together with that pastor for the good of the kingdom of God. Never should one work only for his or her own personal gain or good. We should support one another's endeavors, differences, and personal boundaries. We should work together for the cause and glory of Jesus Christ and His church, which is never stopped or defined by lines of local church affiliation.

Love God, love the truth, love people, and love unity and cooperation. These will assist every minister in keeping his or her obligations to the body of Jesus Christ.

Minister's Ethics toward Organizational Leadership

Do we have ethical responsibilities toward the leaders of our church organization? Yes, we absolutely do.

First, we owe organizational leaders the same ethical treatment we owe to all people. We owe them fundamental love, respect, and interactions rooted in ethical integrity. Beyond those basics, however, we have other ethical obligations toward leaders. Before further delineating other ethical obligations, however, we need to understand the leadership position of organizational leaders. Consider the following points:

- The body of ministers elects various organizational leaders to serve the organization, leading the structured departmental efforts of the entire body (national, district, sectional, or other).
- The leaders are elected or appointed to serve a term of leadership, after which their term ends. The body may return them to the position for another term, but it is strictly up to the will of the body as the members operate under the general constitution.
- The organizational leaders are given delegated authority to lead the departmental efforts, but they do not have pastoral authority over the ministerial body. They must work among the ministers by building consensus, not through dictatorial fiat. Wise leaders will work through the influencers among the ministers with whom they

are working. They work to get those influencers to buy into their initiatives and then "sell" the idea from the grassroots level of the ministerial body.

- God sanctions the authority structure of organizational leadership, but there is not one exclusive person through whom God will work in each organizational position. The ministerial body elects them to serve the body of ministers in the organized efforts to serve God. Whom the body elects is up to the ministers who are voting; God will work through and with the individuals the ministers elect.

With those points in mind, the leaders need always to remember they serve God, but they also serve the body of the church, both ministers and laity. The ministers who elected them for whatever reason may not reelect them. It is not personal; it is the business of the church organization. The leaders do not "possess" their offices; they only "serve" from and through their offices. When their time of leadership passes, they will return to other endeavors of ministry within the organization, not necessarily in a leadership position.

Leaders who become possessive of their positions place themselves in great jeopardy for the day they are no longer returned to office. Some have become cynical and bitter, somehow feeling cheated by the organizational body when they were not reelected to office. It was always the prerogative of the ministerial body as to who would fill the leadership positions. They must never forget that, and they always should lead to the best of their ability with humility and kindness toward those whom they serve.

I remember a conference in which a minister was stepping down from the leadership position he held, which forced the constituency to fill that particular office with someone else. Because of one minister's particular office of support to the position being vacated, that minister was a logical consideration as one who could move up to the vacated position. However, the electing body did not move in that direction; they chose another to fill the position. The one particular minister who had apparently expected to be elevated in his position of leadership, was visibly shaken and probably disappointed. I watched a dark cloud pass across the minister's face, and frankly, what I witnessed frightened me. Over the next few years, I watched that minister become more and more detached, and soon he departed completely from the Apostolic message. It appeared that bitterness over one election destroyed him over the brief period of time that ensued. We must never become possessive of elected or appointed positions of leadership. They do not belong to the people who fill them; they belong to the church organization.

The ministerial body, in turn, should respect the individuals who have been elected to positions of leadership. Some may be tempted to say, "But I didn't vote for that person. Why should I respect him or her?" The person was elected by the will of the ministerial constituency, therefore the body has an obligation to give the individual honor, respect, and cooperation. As long as a minister belongs to the organization, he or she has a responsibility to work in harmony with its elected leadership. They should

• love and respect their leaders,
• pray for their leaders,

- cooperate with their leaders,
- cooperate with the organized plan of the department, and
- support the organizational leaders.

What other ethical obligations do ministers have with their organization and organizational leaders? They are to cooperate and work together with the body of ministers for the purpose of having a united organizational effort for the cause of Jesus Christ.

Ministers are obligated to pay their ministerial tithing or dues as directed by their member district. Would a pastor appreciate laypersons in the church he or she pastors withholding their tithing? That pastor also should pay tithes, whether it is called tithing or ministerial dues. The pastor owes his or her district the courtesy of cooperation financially through payment of tithing/dues and giving to departmental offerings.

There also are expenses for the upkeep of district-held properties, as well as other financial needs within the district. Pastors rely on their local church members to pay the bills at the local church, and the district leadership relies on its pastors and churches to pay district bills.

There are other areas in which ministers should cooperate with the efforts of the district and organizational leadership. District and national meetings and evangelistic endeavors require the support of the district or national membership. A minister is obligated to do his or her part to support the efforts of the district, section, or general bodies to which he or she belongs.

There also are rules of conduct and membership with which the ministers have a responsibility to cooperate. These rules were developed through the years by the ministerial constituency of the district or general organization. They are meant for the unification and cooperation of the entire district or ministerial constituency, and every member minister has a responsibility to support them.

The minister has ethical obligations the same as every other Christian. He has responsibilities toward his or her community, laypersons, fellow ministers, and the church organization. If he or she will do his or her part to be completely ethical, the world will be a better place to live. There will be more unity and harmony in every area of life. There will be less conflict and hurt feelings, and every individual will feel an important part of the body of Jesus Christ, the church. It all begins with individuals doing what is right, living according to the basic principles of the Scriptures that guide and instruct our conduct. It is all a matter of following the principles of Christian ethics.

A LIFESTYLE THAT HONORS JESUS CHRIST AND AVOIDS REPROACH

Perhaps this entire study could be summed up in one exceptionally brief comment. The essence of Christian ethics is living a life that honors Jesus Christ and does not bring a reproach upon His name or His church.

It has been stated in this book, but it bears one final repeating. Christian ethics involves treating people as we would want to be treated. It is following what is commonly known as the Golden Rule. We should hit the pause button long enough to consider our own feelings and desires for how we prefer to be treated. We then would know how to treat others and could treat them with a high measure of Christian ethics.

It is too easy to distance ourselves from the feelings and concerns of others and think only of ourselves in a situation. But selfishness is at the root of much that is wrong in this world. We ought to break free from our self-centered world long enough to recognize there are people on this earth other than ourselves who also have value to Christ. He loves them like He loves us. Would Jesus want us to treat them less fairly or less kindly than we would want to be treated? And how has Jesus treated us? It is only right we treat others with the same kindness, love, and respect.

Glen Campbell, a popular singer of the 1970s, recorded the song "Try a Little Kindness," written by Curt Sapaugh and Bobby Austin, and the song became a hit on three different music charts. If we would live by the principle of kindness toward others, what a better world this could be!

When I turned fifteen I had been attending a Pentecostal church for only a short time. The month after I received the Holy Spirit, my Sunday school teacher, Nell Tippy, gave me a book for my birthday. It is the book I prize most among all the volumes in my library—*In His Steps* by Charles M. Sheldon. The premise of the book is simple yet powerful. The main pastor-character of the book challenged his congregation: "Before doing anything, ask yourself the question, 'What would Jesus do?'"

In conclusion, I leave you with the same challenge when wrestling with ethical considerations. Take a moment to contemplate, "What would Jesus do?" If you will but consider those four words, I believe you will know how to act and react ethically in every situation that arises.